easy 30-minute meals

easy 30-minute meals

quick and easy recipes for busy people

RYLAND
PETERS
& SMALL

LONDON NEW YORK

Designer Paul Stradling

Editor Ellen Parnavelas

Production Manager Gordana Simakovic

Art Director Leslie Harrington

Editorial Director Julia Charles

Indexer Hilary Bird

First published in 2012
by Ryland Peters & Small
20–21 Jockey's Fields
London WC1R 4BW
and
Ryland Peters & Small, Inc.
519 Broadway, 5th Floor
New York, NY10012

www.rylandpeters.com

ISBN UK: 978 1 84975 209 1
10 9 8 7 6 5 4 3 2 1

ISBN US: 978 1 84975 210 7
10 9 8 7 6 5 4 3 2 1

Text © Ross Dobson, Caroline Marson, Lindy
Wildsmith, Fiona Smith, Tonia George, Jennie
Shapter, Fran Warde, Louise Pickford, Silvana
Franco, Vatcharin Bhumichitr, Nadia Arumugam,
Kimiko Barber, Ghillie Basan, Hannah Miles, Laura
Washburn, Kate Habershon, Lyndel Costain
and Ryland Peters & Small 2012

Design and photographs
© Ryland Peters & Small 2012

Printed in China

Notes
• All spoon measurements are level unless
otherwise specified.

• Weights and measurements have been
rounded up or down slightly to make
measuring easier.

• Eggs are medium unless otherwise specified.
Uncooked or partly cooked eggs should not
be served to the very young, the very old,
those with compromised immune systems or
to pregnant women.

• Ovens should be preheated to the specified
temperature. Recipes in this book were tested
using a regular oven. If using a fan-assisted
oven, follow the manufacturer's instructions
for adjusting temperatures.

• When a recipe calls for the grated zest of
citrus fruit, buy unwaxed fruit and wash well
before using. If you can only find treated fruit,
scrub well in warm soapy water and rinse
before using.

contents

introduction

In today's fast-paced world, busy people are always looking for new ways to make quick and delicious home-cooked meals. With Easy 30-minute Meals, making good food in a flash just got easier. This handy book is bursting with ideas for main meals and desserts, each of which take about 30 minutes to prepare and cook.

Whether it's a substantial salad for a lunch on the go, a comforting soup for a cold winter's night, a speedy stir-fry to use up those leftovers or a hearty family dinner, this book has all the recipes you need to get a meal on the table in minutes. Tuck into a substantial Salad and you'll feel satisfied. Try a Salad Niçoise with Fresh Tuna or a Mexican Taco Salad. Soups are so versatile, there's something for everyone – try a nutritious Grilled Salmon Noodle Soup or a hearty Smoked Haddock and Bean Soup. Eggs are an easy, super-quick option for everyone in the family, including vegetarians. Tortilla with Potatoes and Roasted Pimentos or Tortilla with Artichokes and Serrano Ham can be served at any time of day.

A bowl of Pasta with your favourite sauce and a generous helping of grated cheese is hard to beat. Try Penne with Spicy Meatballs for a delicious Italian classic. There are plenty of Stir-fries to choose from, whether you like yours spicy, meaty, vegetarian, light or substantial. Options include Buddha's Delight and Gingered Chicken Noodles. For all those who like nothing better than Family Favourites, this chapter will tick all the boxes; from Wild Salmon and Sorrel Cakes to Spicy Sausage and Pepper Pizza. Finally, not even a shortage of time should stand in the way of a sweet treat. Desserts include Roasted Mascarpone Peaches and Spiced Pear Trifle.

Easy 30-minute Meals is packed with inspiration for fuss-free food. Perfect for busy people, it will soon become your go-to book for tasty, effortless recipes.

salads

roasted pepper & aubergine salad

1 tablespoon pine nuts

150 g/2 cups mixed salad leaves (such as Italian-style)

100 g/½ cup chargrilled bell peppers, sliced

100 g/½ cup roasted aubergines/eggplant, sliced

50 g/1¾ oz. feta or firm goat cheese, sliced

a handful of fresh basil leaves, shredded

2 tablespoons extra virgin olive oil

freshly ground black pepper

Italian bread, to serve

serves 2

This light salad is simplicity itself to prepare. All you need to do is use the best-quality ingredients you can find. Look out at the deli counter for chargrilled red and yellow peppers and roasted or grilled aubergines/eggplant, but if you can't find them, use ones that are preserved in oil and sold in jars.

First toast the pine nuts. Spread out a tablespoonful (or more if toasting a batch) in a thin layer on the base of a large, non-stick frying pan and place over low heat. Cook over low to medium heat for 2–3 minutes, tossing them frequently until they are golden brown. Remove from the heat and set aside until needed.

Put the salad leaves, peppers, aubergines/eggplant, toasted pine nuts, cheese and shredded basil in a large bowl. Add the olive oil, season well with pepper and toss to coat.

Arrange the salad on serving plates and serve immediately with a basket of good-quality Italian bread, such as ciabatta or Pugliese.

Variation: Add a few slices of Parma ham and some pitted black olives to the salad.

beetroot, walnut & warm goat cheese salad

Pomegranate molasses is a thick, sticky liquid made from reduced pomegranate juice that is used in Middle Eastern cooking. If you can't get hold of pomegranate molasses, use a good, thick, syrupy balsamic vinegar or reduce a thinner vinegar slowly in a small pan until it has halved in volume.

To make the dressing, mix together the pomegranate molasses or balsamic vinegar, walnut oil, orange juice and garlic in a bowl. Pour over the beetroot/beets and season with salt and pepper to taste. Cover and leave to marinate for 20 minutes.

Meanwhile, preheat the grill/broiler to medium. Lightly toast one side of the ciabatta bread under the grill/broiler. Turn the bread over and arrange the goat cheese on the other side. Grill/broil for a further 3–4 minutes, or until the top begins to turn golden.

Arrange the salad leaves and walnuts on serving plates, top with the marinated beetroot/beets and goat cheese toasts and pour over the remaining dressing. Serve immediately.

2 tablespoons pomegranate molasses or balsamic vinegar

1 tablespoon walnut oil

freshly squeezed juice of 1 orange

1 garlic clove, crushed

200 g/7 oz. cooked fresh beetroot/beets (not pickled), quartered

4 thick slices ciabatta bread

100 g/1 cup firm goat cheese, crumbled

100 g/1¼ cups mixed salad leaves

50 g/½ cup walnut halves

sea salt and freshly ground black pepper

serves 2

warm cherry tomato & mozzarella salad

500 g/5 cups pasta, such as farfalle or small fat tubetti

200 g/2 cups baby mozzarella cheeses, drained and halved

250 g/1¼ cups halved cherry tomatoes

4 tablespoons good olive oil

50 g rocket/arugula

extra virgin olive oil

balsamic vinegar

sea salt and freshly ground black pepper

serves 4–6

This warm salad is the perfect dish for alfresco eating. Try adding some toasted pine nuts or finely chopped garlic and fresh herbs.

Bring a large saucepan of water to the boil, add plenty of salt and return to the boil. Cook the pasta according to the package instructions and set aside.

Put the mozzarella and cherry tomatoes in a large bowl. Add the olive oil, season with salt and pepper to taste, then mix to combine.

Add the hot pasta to the mozzarella salad and mix well. Add the rocket/arugula, turn once, then spoon onto a flat serving dish. Sprinkle with olive oil and balsamic vinegar and serve warm.

Variation: Add toasted pine nuts (see page 10) or finely chopped garlic to the mozzarella and tomatoes. Finely chop 2 handfuls parsley, mint and basil, and use instead of the rocket/arugula.

Italian tuna & bean salad

Fresh tuna can be expensive, so this recipe is a good way of making one wonderful steak stretch a little further. White cannellini beans are more traditional, but using green flageolet beans makes this colourful dish even more vibrant.

Preheat a grill pan/griddle or frying pan over high heat.

If using fresh tuna, brush with olive oil and season with salt and pepper. Add to the preheated pan and cook for 3 minutes on each side or until barred with brown but pink in the middle (depending on the thickness of the fish). Remove from the pan, leave to cool and then pull into chunks.

Put the oil, onions, crushed garlic and vinegar in a bowl and beat with a fork. Add the beans and toss to coat.

Add the tuna and basil, salt and pepper, then serve immediately with crusty bread.

1 large tuna steak, about 250 g/9 oz., or 2 small cans good-quality tuna, about 160 g/5¾ oz. each, drained

6 tablespoons olive oil, plus extra for brushing

2 red onions, finely sliced

2–3 fat garlic cloves, crushed

1 tablespoon sherry vinegar or white wine vinegar

2 x 400-g/14-oz. cans green flageolet beans, white cannellini beans, or a mixture of both

4 handfuls of fresh basil leaves and small sprigs

sea salt and freshly ground black pepper

crusty bread, to serve

serves 4–6

pasta salad with roasted peppers, olives & feta

1 red bell pepper

1 yellow bell pepper

3 tablespoons light olive oil

2 teaspoons fresh thyme leaves

1 handful of fresh flaf-leaf parsley, roughly chopped

1 handful of small basil leaves

80 g/½ cup kalamata olives, halved

400 g/4 cups wholemeal/wheat penne, or similar pasta

150 g/1½ cups feta cheese, crumbled

sea salt and freshly ground black pepper

serves 4

Here a number of typically Mediterranean flavours are served with a nutty wholemeal/wheat pasta. Marinated feta would also work well here, adding to the salad's warm and sunny feel.

Preheat the oven to 220°C (425°F) Gas 7.

Brush the peppers with 1 tablespoon of the oil, place on a baking sheet and cook in the preheated oven for 15 minutes, turning often until they puff up and blacken evenly all over.

Remove the peppers from the oven and put them in a plastic food bag. When cool enough to handle, remove the skin, stalks, seeds and any membranes and thinly slice the remaining flesh. Put the slices in a large bowl and add the remaining oil, herbs and olives. Cover and set aside for 10 minutes to allow the flavours to develop.

Bring a large saucepan of water to the boil, add plenty of salt and return to the boil. Cook the pasta according to the package instructions. When the pasta is cooked, drain and refresh with cold water to cool a little and add to the other ingredients. Use your hands to mix well. Season with salt and pepper, add the feta and toss to combine. Serve immediately.

hot smoked salmon & cannellini bean salad with gremolata

Gremolata is a zesty mixture of parsley, lemon zest and garlic, sometimes combined with olive oil, which is used in many classic Italian dishes. Here it is used to balance the richness of hot smoked salmon. The addition of buttery cannellini beans makes this a delicious and satisfying salad.

Combine the parsley, mint, garlic, lemon zest and juice and oil in a small bowl.

Roughly flake the salmon into a large bowl and add the beans, onions, cucumber and spinach leaves. Season to taste with salt and pepper and toss to combine. Serve immediately with the gremolata on the side as a spooning sauce.

Vegetarian option: Replace the salmon with 400 g/8 oz. firm tofu or tempeh (an Indonesian speciality that has a nuttier, more savoury flavour than tofu), cut into thin strips, and add a handful of roughly chopped fresh coriander/cilantro for extra flavour.

leaves from a bunch of fresh
flat-leaf parsley, roughly chopped

leaves from a bunch of fresh mint,
roughly chopped

1 garlic clove, crushed

1 teaspoon finely grated lemon zest

2 tablespoons freshly squeezed
lemon juice

65 ml/4 tablespoons extra virgin
olive oil

400 g/8 oz. hot smoked salmon fillet

1 x 410-g/14-oz. can cannellini beans,
drained and well rinsed

2 small red onions, thinly sliced

1 cucumber, peeled, split lengthwise,
deseeded and sliced into crescents

50 g/scant 1 cup baby spinach leaves

sea salt and freshly ground
black pepper

serves 4

pea, prosciutto & pasta salad

350 g/3½ cups pasta shape of
your choice, such as orecchiette,
fusilli or farfalle

1 tablespoon olive oil

1 large onion, finely chopped

2 garlic cloves, crushed

100 g/3½ oz. prosciutto or
bacon slices

350 g/2⅓ cups frozen or fresh peas

2 tablespoons extra virgin olive oil

2 tablespoons white wine vinegar

1 teaspoon Dijon mustard

2 tablespoons fresh flat-leaf parsley,
chopped

2 tablespoons fresh chervil or
tarragon, chopped

2 tablespoons chopped mint

sea salt and freshly ground
black pepper

serves 6

*This is an elegant and light twist on a traditional pasta salad.
You can either use frozen peas or make the most of the tender
sweetness of fresh peas when they are in season.*

Bring a large saucepan of water to the boil, add plenty of salt
and return to the boil. Cook the pasta of your choice according to
the package instructions.

While the pasta is cooking, heat the olive oil in a frying pan over
medium heat. Add the onion and garlic and cook for 5 minutes. Add
the prosciutto and cook for a further 5 minutes. Add the peas, cover
and cook gently for 5 minutes until the peas are tender. (Remember
that fresh peas will need slightly less cooking time.)

In a bowl, mix together the extra virgin olive oil, vinegar and
mustard to make the dressing. Season with salt and pepper to taste.

When the pasta is cooked, drain and refresh with cold water to
cool a little. Combine the pasta with the pea and prosciutto mixture,
dressing, parsley, chervil and mint and toss to coat. Arrange the
salad on serving plates and serve immediately.

Mexican taco salad with pinto beans & avocado

The fresh flavours of tomato, avocado and coriander/cilantro form the basis of Mexican cuisine and are combined here in a nutritious salad with pinto beans and crunchy taco pieces. If you want a dressing, simply add a little good olive oil combined with freshly squeezed lime juice.

Preheat the oven to 180°C (350°F) Gas 4.

Cut the avocados in half and remove the stones. Use a tablespoon to scoop out the flesh in one piece and slice it into wedges. Put it in a large bowl with the beans.

Cut the tomatoes in half, squeeze out and discard as many seeds as possible and thinly slice the flesh. Put in the bowl with the beans and avocados. Add the olives, onion, coriander/cilantro and lettuce and gently toss to combine.

Put the taco shells on a baking sheet and cook in the preheated oven for 8–10 minutes, until crisp. When cool enough to handle, roughly break each taco shell into pieces and add to the bowl of salad. Gently toss to combine, being careful not to break up the taco pieces, and serve immediately.

2 firm, ripe avocados

150 g/2½ cups canned pinto or kidney beans

3 ripe tomatoes

50 g/scant ⅓ cup stoned black olives, sliced

1 red onion, thinly sliced

leaves from a small bunch of fresh coriander/cilantro, roughly chopped

1 crisp lettuce, shredded

8 stoneground yellow corn taco shells (preferably organic)

serves 4

bacon, egg & bean salad with grilled chorizo on toast

250 g/1¼ cups fresh or 500 g/2½ cups frozen broad/fava beans

200 g/7 oz. bacon slices

6 eggs, at room temperature

3 tablespoons freshly squeezed lemon juice

½ teaspoon sugar

¼ teaspoon sea salt

freshly ground black pepper

6 tablespoons extra virgin olive oil

200 g/scant 3 cups baby spinach leaves, washed

6 chorizo sausages

6 slices of crusty bread, such as ciabatta, toasted

serves 6

This hearty salad is really just a healthier version of a mixed grill – perfect for a speedy lunch or dinner. If you are using young, tender broad/fava beans, there is no need to peel them.

Bring a large saucepan of water to the boil and add the broad/fava beans. Return the water to the boil, and cook the beans for 2 minutes until tender. Drain, refresh with cold water and peel if necessary.

Heat a frying pan to medium, add the bacon and cook until crisp. Cut into pieces and set aside.

Fill a saucepan with water, add the eggs and bring to the boil. Continue to boil for 4 minutes for medium and 6 minutes for hard-boiled/hard-cooked, as preferred. Drain and refresh with cold water. When cool enough to handle, peel and set aside.

In a large bowl, whisk together the lemon juice, sugar, salt, pepper and oil and set aside. Add the spinach and toss to coat. Set aside.

Preheat the grill/broiler to hot. Cut the chorizo into slices and put under the hot grill/broiler for 5 minutes, turning once, until heated through.

Arrange the dressed spinach, broad/fava beans and bacon on serving plates. Cut the eggs into halves or quarters and place on the plates. Top each piece of toast with the chorizo slices and serve immediately with the salad.

lemon-rubbed lamb
& orzo pasta salad

This colourful salad can be made well ahead of time; just cook and add the lamb before serving. With lemon, tomatoes and fresh basil, it's full of the flavours of summer. If orzo is difficult to find, you can use mini pasta shells or macaroni instead.

Preheat the oven to 220°C (425°F) Gas 7.

In a small bowl, combine the garlic and lemon zest with 1 tablespoon of the oil and season with salt and pepper. Rub this over the lamb and set aside until needed.

Preheat the grill/broiler to hot. Put the lamb under the grill/broiler and cook for 2 minutes each side, then transfer to a roasting pan and cook in the preheated oven for 5 minutes for medium rare or up to 10 minutes for more well done. Remove from the oven, wrap in foil and leave to rest for 10 minutes.

Cut the peppers into thick strips, discarding the stems and seeds. Cook under the hot grill/broiler until tender. Set aside.

Bring a large saucepan of water to the boil, add plenty of salt and return to the boil. Cook the orzo according to the package instructions. Drain and toss with the remaining 2 tablespoons oil, lemon juice, peppers, cherry tomatoes, artichokes, onion and pesto. Season with salt and pepper to taste.

Arrange the salad on a serving platter. Slice the lamb and arrange it on top of the salad. Scatter with the pine nuts and basil leaves and serve immediately.

3 garlic cloves, crushed

finely grated zest of 2 lemons and freshly squeezed juice of 1

3 tablespoons olive oil

300-g/10½-oz. piece of lean lamb fillet

1 large red bell pepper

1 large yellow bell pepper

250 g/1 cup orzo pasta

20 cherry tomatoes

400-g/14-oz. can or jar artichoke hearts, drained and quartered

1 small red onion, thinly sliced

4 tablespoons fresh or bottled pesto

4 tablespoons pine nuts, toasted (see page 10)

leaves from a small bunch of fresh basil

sea salt and freshly ground black pepper

serves 4

salade niçoise with fresh tuna

8 small waxy potatoes

4 eggs

200 g/1¼ cups green beans, trimmed

4 x 160-g/5½ oz. tuna steaks

2 teaspoons olive oil

150 g/2 cups crisp lettuce

4 tomatoes, cut into wedges

16 black olives

2 tablespoons white wine vinegar

1 teaspoon Dijon mustard

4 tablespoons extra virgin olive oil

sea salt and freshly ground black pepper

serves 4

Salade Niçoise is traditionally made with canned tuna, but fresh tuna steaks make it extra special and more filling. Of course you can always use good-quality canned or bottled tuna if you prefer.

Put the potatoes in a large saucepan of water and bring to the boil. Reduce the heat and cook until tender. Drain and refresh with cold water. When cool enough to handle, halve or quarter if necessary.

Fill a saucepan with water, add the eggs and bring to the boil. Continue to boil for 4 minutes for medium and 6 minutes for hard-boiled/hard-cooked, as preferred. Drain and refresh with cold water. When cool enough to handle, peel and quarter and set aside.

Bring a saucepan of water to the boil, add the beans and cook until tender. Drain and refresh with cold water.

Preheat a grill pan/griddle or frying pan over high heat. Brush the tuna with olive oil and season with salt and pepper. Add to the preheated pan and cook for 3 minutes on each side or until barred with brown but pink in the middle (depending on the thickness of the fish). Remove from the pan then leave to rest for 5 minutes. Cut into pieces.

Arrange the lettuce, tomatoes, olives, potatoes, egg quarters, beans and tuna on serving plates.

In a bowl, whisk together the vinegar and mustard and season with salt and pepper. Whisk in the olive oil until well blended. Pour over each salad and serve immediately.

pork & lentil salad

This is a hearty and delicious salad. The Puy lentils give a lovely nutty texture and a rustic feel to the dish.

Fill a large saucepan with water, add the lentils and bring to the boil. Reduce to a simmer and cook for 20 minutes. Drain and set aside.

In a large bowl, whisk together the mustard, vinegar and ¼ teaspoon each of salt and pepper, then whisk in the extra virgin olive oil. Add the mushrooms and warm lentils and toss well to coat. Set aside to marinate.

In a small bowl, mix together the olive oil, lemon zest, garlic, rosemary and remaining ¼ teaspoon each of salt and pepper. Rub this mixture all over the pork fillets.

Heat a frying pan to medium, add the pork and cook for 5 minutes on each side. Remove from the pan and leave to rest on a chopping board for 5 minutes, then slice thinly.

Pour the wine into the hot frying pan and let it bubble, stirring in any leftover marinade. Pour this over the lentils and mushrooms.

Add the sliced pork to the lentils and mushrooms along with the spinach leaves and cherry tomatoes and toss to combine. Arrange the salad on serving plates and serve immediately.

200 g/1 cup dried Puy or French green lentils

1 teaspoon Dijon mustard

2 tablespoons balsamic vinegar

½ teaspoon sea salt

½ teaspoon freshly ground black pepper

4 tablespoons extra virgin olive oil

250 g/2 cups button mushrooms

1 tablespoon olive oil

finely grated zest of 1 lemon

2 garlic cloves, crushed

2 tablespoons leaves from a sprig of fresh rosemary

350-g/12-oz. piece of pork tenderloin/ eye fillet

100 ml/⅓ cup red wine

100 g/1¼ cups baby spinach leaves, washed

16 cherry tomatoes, halved

serves 4

tabbouleh with chickpeas & spring salad

90 g fine bulgur wheat

2 tablespoons freshly squeezed lemon juice

60 ml/4 tablespoons extra virgin olive oil

1 small bunch of fresh flat-leaf parsley, finely chopped

1 large handful of fresh mint leaves, finely chopped

2 tablespoons fresh dill, finely chopped

1 small punnet/basket of cherry tomatoes, halved

1 x 400-g/14-oz. can chickpeas, rinsed and drained

120–150 g/2 cups mixed salad leaves

sea salt and freshly ground black pepper

lemon wedges, to serve

serves 4

This fresh-tasting salad is made with bulgur wheat. This is cracked wheat and may be one of man's first attempts at processing food. Simply cover with boiling water to soften and add to your favourite salad ingredients.

Put the bulgur wheat in a heatproof bowl and pour over 125 ml/ ½ cup boiling water. Stir once, cover with plastic wrap and leave to swell for 8–10 minutes. Put the lemon juice and olive oil in a small bowl and whisk. Pour over the bulgur wheat and stir well with a fork, fluffing up the bulgur wheat and separating the grains.

Put the bulgur wheat in a large bowl with the parsley, mint, dill, tomatoes, chickpeas and salad leaves. Toss to combine and season well with salt and pepper. Arrange the salad on serving plates and serve immediately with lemon wedges.

warm chicken livers with watercress & ciabatta

To make a meat-free version of this salad, simply replace the livers with quartered mushrooms. Or, for an extra-rich salad, add a handful of chopped, crispy bacon.

Heat 1 tablespoon of the olive oil over medium-low heat in a large frying pan. Add the onion and cook for 10 minutes until soft and turning golden. Set aside.

Preheat the grill/broiler to hot. Brush the ciabatta with 1 tablespoon of the olive oil and grill/broil until brown on both sides. Tear into bite-sized pieces. Arrange on serving plates with the watercress.

Carefully sort through the livers, cutting off any green specks of bile and pulling away sinew and connective tissue, then rinse.

Heat the remaining olive oil in the frying pan and add the livers. Cook for 3 minutes, stirring, until just done. Transfer the livers to a warmed plate. Add the Marsala to the pan and bring to the boil. Let boil for 1 minute, scraping the pan and stirring until the mixture has reduced by half.

Return the livers to the pan with the mustard, sage and a little salt and pepper, and toss in the pan for 30 seconds.

Pile the hot livers and onion on top of the watercress and ciabatta. Drizzle with a little extra virgin olive oil and serve immediately.

3 tablespoons olive oil

1 onion, thinly sliced

6 slices of ciabatta bread

500 g/6½ cups watercress, thick stems removed

500 g/1 lb 2 oz. chicken livers, halved

125 ml/½ cup Marsala or cream sherry

1 tablespoon wholegrain mustard

1 tablespoon fresh sage, chopped

sea salt and freshly ground black pepper

extra virgin olive oil, for drizzling

serves 4

couscous with feta, dill & spring beans

275 g/1¼ cups couscous

5 tablespoons extra virgin olive oil

1 garlic clove, peeled and crushed

3 shallots, peeled and thinly sliced

2 tablespoons fresh dill, chopped

2 tablespoons fresh chives, chopped

1 tablespoon finely chopped preserved lemon, or 1 tablespoon zest and flesh of fresh lemon, finely chopped

250 g/2½ cups feta cheese, chopped

150 g/1 cup mangetout/snow peas

150 g/1 cup frozen baby broad/fava beans, defrosted

150 g/1 cup frozen peas, defrosted

freshly ground black pepper

serves 4

Dill is a floral, grassy herb and the scent of it conjures up springtime, which is why it is so perfectly complemented by the beans and peas in this dish. Marinating the feta lifts it from a salty, creamy cheese to something much more complex, so it's well worth it, even if it's just for 5 minutes.

Put the couscous in a heatproof bowl and pour over 400 ml/1½ cups boiling water. Cover with plastic wrap or a plate and leave to swell for 10 minutes.

Pour the olive oil into a mixing bowl and add the garlic, shallots, dill, chives, preserved lemon and lots of pepper. Add the feta and set aside while you cook the beans.

Bring a saucepan of water to the boil. Add the mangetout/snow peas, and cook for 1 minute. Add the broad/fava beans and cook for another minute. Finally, add the peas, cook for 2 minutes and drain.

Uncover the couscous, stir in the hot beans, transfer to bowls and top with the feta, spooning over the flavoured oil as you go. Stir well before serving.

soups

flag bean soup

This is the sort of soup you need on a cold winter's day. Using canned beans, it takes no time at all to prepare, and you can use vegetable or chicken stock, according to whether your audience is vegetarian or not.

Heat the oil in a frying pan, add the sliced garlic and fry gently on both sides until crisp and golden. Remove from the pan and drain on paper towels.

Add the onion and crushed garlic to the frying pan, with some extra oil if necessary, and cook over medium heat until softened and transparent. Add the lentils and half the boiling stock and cook until the lentils are just tender.

Meanwhile, rinse and drain all the beans. Put them in a sieve/ strainer then immerse in a large saucepan of boiling water to reheat them.

Add the hot beans to the lentils and pour in the remaining stock. Season with salt and pepper to taste. If the soup is too thick, add extra boiling stock or water. Ladle into bowls, top with the reserved fried garlic and the herbs, add a few drops of basil oil and serve immediately with crusty bread.

1 tablespoon olive oil, plus extra to taste

3 large garlic cloves, 2 cut into slices, 1 crushed

1 large onion, finely chopped

250 g/1¼ cups dried Puy or French green lentils

1 litre/4 cups boiling chicken or vegetable stock, plus extra to taste

100 g/1¼ cups canned butter/ lima beans

200 g/3½ cups canned green flageolet beans

200 g/3½ cups canned red kidney beans

200 g/3½ cups canned haricot or cannellini beans

sea salt and freshly ground black pepper

to serve

leaves from a bunch of fresh flat-leaf parsley

basil oil or olive oil, for drizzling

crusty bread

serves 4

chicken, lemongrass, ginger & rice soup

50 g/¼ cup Basmati rice

500 ml/2 cups chicken stock

1½ tablespoons light soy sauce

½ teaspoon dried chilli/hot pepper flakes

½ lemongrass stalk, outer leaves removed, finely chopped

½-cm/⅛-inch piece of fresh ginger, peeled and finely chopped

2 garlic cloves, thinly sliced

3 chicken breasts (each about 150 g/ 5½ oz.), cut into small pieces

1 red bell pepper, thinly sliced

3 spring onions/scallions, finely chopped

50 g/½ cup Chinese cabbage, finely shredded (optional)

a squeeze of fresh lime juice

freshly ground black pepper

a handful of fresh coriander/ cilantro leaves, to garnish

serves 2–4

This oriental rice soup can be enjoyed as a snack at any time, but it's sustaining enough to make a light meal. For the best flavour, look out for ready-made fresh chicken stock – or, better still, when you cook a chicken, make a batch of stock for the freezer.

Cook the rice according to the package instructions. Drain, rinse, and set aside until needed.

Heat the stock to boiling point in a large pan. Add the soy sauce, dried chilli/hot pepper flakes, lemongrass, ginger and garlic, and cook over high heat for 5 minutes.

Add the chicken pieces and red pepper and let the mixture gently bubble for about 3 minutes, or until the chicken is tender.

Add the cooked rice and cook for a further 1 minute. Finally, stir in the spring onions/scallions and cabbage (if using). Ladle into warmed serving bowls. Squeeze a little lime juice over each, season with pepper and garnish with coriander/cilantro leaves. Serve immediately.

Variation: This soup also works well using shelled uncooked prawns/shrimp. Simply substitute them for the chicken and cook in the same way. Add a handful of spinach leaves at the end.

fresh pea soup with mint & crispy bacon

One of the great classics of the soup world is pea and ham soup. This modern variation uses crispy bacon instead of ham and can be made with frozen peas for added convenience.

Heat the oil in a frying pan over medium heat, add the pancetta and cook until crisp. Remove and drain on crumpled paper towels, or drape over a wooden spoon so they curl.

Bring a saucepan of water to the boil. Add the peas and cook for 2–3 minutes or until tender. Drain.

Bring the stock to the boil in a saucepan. Transfer the peas to a blender and add 1–2 ladles of stock. Work to a purée, adding extra stock if necessary. Add the remaining stock and blend again. Taste and adjust the seasoning. Reheat, thinning with a little boiling water if necessary, then ladle into warmed serving bowls and serve immediately, topped with the crisp bacon, a swirl of cream and a few sprigs of fresh mint.

1 tablespoon olive oil

4–8 slices very thinly cut smoked pancetta or smoked bacon slices

500 g/3⅓ cups shelled peas, fresh or frozen

1 litre/4 cups ham, chicken or vegetable stock

sea salt and freshly ground black pepper

to serve

4 tablespoons single/light cream

a few sprigs of fresh mint

serves 4

summer vegetable soup with pasta & pistou

2 tablespoons light olive oil

6 baby leeks, finely sliced

2 courgettes/zucchini, diced

2 small yellow pattypan squash

1 small fennel bulb, diced

1 litre/4 cups vegetable stock

100 g/^{2}/$_3$ cup young pea pods

100 g/1^1/$_3$ cups fresh broad/ fava beans, shelled if necessary

50 g/^{1}/$_2$ cup fresh pasta shapes of your choice

finely grated Parmesan, to serve

pistou

4 garlic cloves, chopped

^{1}/$_2$ teaspoon sea salt

2 tomatoes, skinned and chopped

100 g/1 cup fresh basil leaves, torn

50 g/^{1}/$_2$ cup fresh flat-leaf parsley leaves

125 ml/^{1}/$_2$ cup olive oil

2 tablespoons freshly squeezed lemon juice

25 g/^{1}/$_4$ cup finely grated Parmesan

serves 4

French pistou is a fragrant paste, similar in style to Italian pesto. The garlic and aromatic herbs are used here to amplify the flavours of this rich vegetable soup. Try and find tender young broad/fava beans for this light, broth-style soup – older beans will have tough skins and need to be shelled.

To make the pistou, put the garlic and salt in a large mortar and pound with a pestle until the garlic forms a smooth paste. Add the tomatoes and pound until smooth. Add the basil and parsley and pound until combined. Slowly add the olive oil until it is all incorporated. Add the lemon juice and Parmesan and stir to combine. Cover and refrigerate until needed.

Heat the light olive oil in a large saucepan over high heat. Add the leeks and cook for 2–3 minutes, stirring constantly. Next, add the courgettes/zucchini, squash and fennel and cook, stirring, for 1–2 minutes until the vegetables soften but keep their colour. Add the stock and bring to the boil. Add the pea pods and broad/fava beans and cook for 5 minutes. Add the pasta to the soup and gently simmer for 1–2 minutes, until it is cooked but still retains a little 'bite'.

Ladle into warmed serving bowls, top with a spoonful of pistou and finely grated Parmesan and serve immediately.

chicken avgolemono

Avgolemono is a family of Mediterranean sauces and soups made with egg and lemon mixed with broth and then heated to thicken. It gives a lovely creamy texture and a delicious citrus taste to this rich and satisfying soup.

Heat the stock in a large saucepan and add the rice. Bring to the boil and simmer for 15 minutes or until the rice is tender. Add the chicken and warm through for 2–3 minutes.

In the meantime, whisk the eggs with the lemon juice in a small bowl. Add a ladleful of the warm stock and whisk until thinned. Remove the soup from the heat and gradually pour in the egg mixture, whisking to amalgamate. It should thicken in the residual heat, but if you need to, place it over low heat for just 3–4 minutes, stirring the bottom of the pan to thicken. Do not return to high heat once the egg has been added, or it will boil and scramble. Season with salt and pepper to taste.

Ladle into warmed serving bowls, garnish with parsley and croutons and serve immediately.

1.4 litres/5¾ cups chicken stock

100 g/½ cup long grain rice

400 g/14 oz. cooked chicken, shredded

3 eggs

freshly squeezed juice of 1 lemon

sea salt and freshly ground black pepper

to serve

a handful of fresh flat-leaf parsley, chopped

ready made croutons

serves 4

grilled salmon noodle soup

350g/12 oz. silken tofu

2 bundles somen or soba noodles

4 large salmon steaks, skin on

2 tablespoons sunflower oil

1 litre/4 cups dashi stock powder
mixed with water

your choice of other vegetables, such
as sugar snap peas (a large handful
per serving)

a handful of Chinese dried mushrooms,
such as tree ear (optional), soaked in
hot water for 20 minutes

about 6 spring onions/scallions, sliced

fish sauce or soy sauce, to taste
(optional)

freshly sliced chillies/chiles (optional)

serves 4

Given some fresh salmon steaks and a kitchen stocked with a few basic Asian ingredients, this elegant dinner dish can be on the table in about 8 minutes.

To prepare the tofu, put it between 2 plates and put a weight on top. This will force out some of the liquid and make it stick together better. Just before serving, cut into about 12 cubes.

Bring a large saucepan of water to the boil. Cook the noodles according to the package instructions. When the noodles are cooked, drain and immerse in cold water until ready to serve.

Put the salmon in a plastic bag, add the oil and toss to coat. Preheat a grill pan/griddle or frying pan over high heat, then add the salmon, skin side down. When the skin is charred and the flesh has turned pale about 1 cm/½ inch through, turn the salmon over and sear the other side.

Bring the dashi to the boil, then lightly blanch your chosen vegetables. Remove with a slotted spoon. Drain the mushrooms and slice into pieces, discarding the hard stalk tip.

Put a pile of drained noodles into each warmed serving bowl and top with the salmon steaks, skin side up. Add the tofu cubes, mushrooms and any other vegetables. Ladle the stock over the top and serve immediately topped with sliced spring onions/scallions, soy or fish sauce and sliced fresh chillies/chiles, if desired.

swiss chard & white bean minestrone

Minestrone is a style of delicious Italian vegetable soup that can really be whatever you want it to be. In this recipe, the soup is made extra hearty by serving it over thick and garlicky toasted ciabatta to mop up all the goodness.

Melt the butter in a saucepan over medium heat until sizzling. Add the onion and cook for 4–5 minutes until soft. Add the Swiss chard and cook for 5 minutes, stirring often, until softened. Add the stock and beans and gently bring to the boil. Season with salt and pepper.

Toast the ciabatta until golden on both sides. Rub the garlic cloves over the toasted bread, then place a slice in each warmed serving bowl. Drizzle each piece of bread with olive oil and ladle over the soup. Sprinkle the Parmesan on top and serve immediately.

Variation: This dish can be made into a satisfying pasta meal. Simply leave out the stock and add 400 g/2 cups cooked pasta shapes to the pan when you add the beans, season with salt and pepper and stir in some finely grated Parmesan for extra flavour.

2 tablespoons butter

1 onion, chopped

1 small bunch of Swiss chard, finely chopped

1 litre/2 cups vegetable stock

1 x 400-g/14-oz. can cannellini beans, drained but not rinsed, and roughly mashed

4 thick slices of ciabatta

2 garlic cloves, peeled and halved

extra virgin olive oil, for drizzling

finely grated Parmesan, to serve

sea salt and freshly ground black pepper

serves 4

tom yum seafood noodle soup

100 g/3½ oz. uncooked large or king
prawns/shrimp, shells on

2 tablespoons tom yum paste

1 fresh red chilli/chile, deseeded
and finely chopped

1 red bell pepper, thinly sliced

100 g/scant 1 cup sliced brown-cap
mushrooms

100 g/1 cup trimmed and
finely diced leeks

100 g/1¼ cups rice noodles

freshly squeezed juice of 1 lime

a handful of fresh coriander/cilantro
sprigs, to garnish

serves 2–4

*This is a wonderful meal-in-a-bowl that takes only minutes to put
together. It is quite spicy, so reduce the quantity of chilli/chile
if you prefer. Tom yum paste is a treasure to have in your
storecupboard for making quick Thai stir-fries or curries.*

Peel the prawns/shrimp and use a very sharp knife to cut each one
along the back so that it opens out like a butterfly (leaving each
prawn/shrimp joined along the base and at the tail). Remove the
black vein.

Bring 570 ml/2¼ cups water to the boil in a large saucepan. Stir in
the tom yum paste until dissolved. Add the chilli/chile, red pepper,
mushrooms and leeks and let simmer for 5 minutes.

Put the noodles in a large heatproof bowl, cover with boiling water
and leave to sit for 3–5 minutes until just tender. Drain and spoon
into deep serving bowls.

Add the prawns/shrimp to the tom yum mixture and simmer for
a further 2–3 minutes. Pour the tum yum soup over the noodles.

Ladle into warmed serving bowls and squeeze a little lime juice
over each bowl. Garnish with sprigs of fresh coriander/cilantro
and serve immediately.

Mediterranean chunky fish stew with cheese toasts

If you have ever tasted the classic French fish soup bouillabaisse and enjoyed the flavour, then this is a good quick version. The combination of saffron, orange and fennel gives the stew its distinctive flavour. If you can't find Noilly Prat, use dry Martini or a dry white wine in its place.

Heat the oil in a saucepan over medium heat. Add the onion, garlic, thyme and fennel and cook for about 6–8 minutes until soft. Add the Noilly Prat, dry Martini or dry white wine and let bubble, uncovered, until the liquid has almost reduced to nothing.

Add the passata, saffron, orange juice and zest and 200 ml/scant 1 cup cold water. Raise the heat and cook for 10 minutes. Add the cod fillet and cook gently for a further 2 minutes, then season with salt and pepper to taste.

Preheat the grill/broiler to hot. Lightly toast the baguette slices on each side under the grill/broiler until golden. Rub the halved garlic over the toasted bread and sprinkle with the grated cheese.

Ladle the stew into warmed serving bowls and balance the cheese-topped toasts on top. Serve immediately.

1 tablespoon olive oil

1 small onion, finely chopped

2 garlic cloves, 1 crushed, 1 peeled and halved

a pinch of dried thyme

125 g/scant 1 cup finely chopped fennel

50 ml/scant ¼ cup Noilly Prat, dry Martini or dry white wine

400 g/1¾ cups passata (Italian sieved tomatoes)

1 pinch of saffron threads

freshly squeezed juice and grated zest of 1 orange

200 g/7 oz. skinless cod fillet, cut into large chunks

4 thin slices of baguette

50 g/½ cup grated Emmental or Gruyère cheese

sea salt and freshly ground black pepper

serves 2

potato, bacon & savoy cabbage soup

2 tablespoons extra virgin olive oil

8 smoked bacon slices

1 onion, chopped

2 garlic cloves, crushed

⅛ teaspoon ground allspice

300 g/1⅔ cups peeled and diced potatoes

¼ savoy cabbage, shredded

400 ml/1⅔ cups chicken stock

400 ml/1⅔ cups whole milk

2 tablespoons fine oatmeal

freshly ground black pepper

serves 4

This recipe was inspired by a Polish soup called zurek that is thickened with a fermented flour batter. Here, oatmeal is used instead, which gives the soup a lovely thick texture.

Heat the oil in a heavy-based saucepan or casserole over high heat. Fry the bacon for 2–3 minutes, until cooked. Turn the heat down and add the onion and garlic. Cover and cook for 3 minutes until soft.

Add the allspice and potatoes, cover and cook for a further 2–3 minutes to start softening the potatoes. Add the cabbage and stir until it has wilted into the rest of the ingredients. Pour in the stock and milk and bring to the boil. Cook until the potatoes are soft.

Mix the oatmeal with 3–4 tablespoons cold water until smooth and gradually whisk into the soup to thicken.

Ladle into warmed serving bowls and serve with a fresh grinding of black pepper.

globe artichoke, tarragon & Roquefort soup

The aromatic flavour of tarragon can be a little overpowering.
It works nicely with the artichokes here, as does the Roquefort,
making this a very special soup.

Bring a large saucepan of water to the boil.

Put the lemon juice and 1.5 litres/6 cups cold water in a large bowl.
Trim the leaves and stems from the artichokes. Cut each head in
half and remove the hairy chokes. As you prepare each one, drop it
in the bowl of water and lemon juice to prevent from discolouring.

When all the artichokes are prepared, add them to the pan of
boiling water. Cook for 10–12 minutes, drain and leave to cool.
When cool enough to handle, trim the artichokes so that you are
left with just the soft, fleshy bits.

Put the oil and butter in a large saucepan over high heat. When the
butter sizzles, add the leek and garlic, partially cover with a lid and
cook for 5 minutes, until the leek softens. Add the tarragon and stir
for 1 minute. Add the stock and bring to the boil. Add the artichokes
and cook for 10 minutes.

Transfer to a blender and purée until smooth, adding extra stock
if necessary. Pour into a clean saucepan over low heat to gently
reheat. Stir in the cream and season with salt and pepper to taste.

Ladle into warmed serving bowls, sprinkle with the Roquefort and
serve immediately.

freshly squeezed juice of 1 lemon

8 large globe artichokes

1 tablespoon olive oil

25 g/2 tablespoons butter

1 large leek, sliced

1 garlic clove, chopped

2 tablespoons fresh tarragon leaves

500 ml/2 cups vegetable stock

125 ml/½ cup single/light cream

100 g/1 cup Roquefort, roughly
crumbled

sea salt and freshly ground black
pepper

serves 4

smoked haddock & bean soup

4 tablespoons extra virgin olive oil

1 red onion, sliced

600 ml/scant 2½ cups fish stock

3 dried bay leaves

finely grated zest of 1 lemon

300 g/10½ oz. smoked haddock, skinned and cubed

1 x 400-g/14-oz. can cannellini beans, drained and rinsed

1 x 400-g/14-oz. can butter/lima beans, drained and rinsed

4 tablespoons crème fraîche or sour cream

sea salt and freshly ground black pepper

serves 4

Smoked haddock provides that warm smoky flavour that cold wintry nights call for. Canned beans are so quick and easy to throw in and thicken soups up nicely.

Heat the oil in a saucepan over medium heat. Add the onion and cook for 10 minutes until soft. Pour in the stock, add the bay leaves and lemon zest and bring to a gentle simmer. Add the smoked haddock and cook for 3–4 minutes until opaque.

Transfer half the cannellini and half the butter/lima beans to a blender and add 200 ml/scant 1 cup water. Work to a purée, adding extra stock if necessary and stir into the soup. Add the remaining whole beans and the crème fraîche and season with salt. Before serving, reheat gently but do not allow to boil.

Ladle into warmed serving bowls and serve immediately with a fresh grinding of black pepper.

sweetcorn & pancetta chowder

This chowder is made with sweetcorn instead of the traditional fish but the principle is still the same – a creamy stock thickened with potatoes and spiked with the rich flavour of smoky bacon.

Heat the butter in a large heavy-based saucepan over medium heat and fry the pancetta until crisp. Turn the heat down and add the onion, carrots and potatoes. Cover and cook gently for 15–20 minutes until soft, stirring occasionally.

Sprinkle the flour into the pan and cook for 1 minute, stirring it into the vegetables. Pour in the milk gradually, blending it with the flour, then add the stock and bay leaves and bring to a gentle simmer. Add the sweetcorn and cook for 5 minutes.

Remove from the heat, stir in the cream and season with salt to taste. Ladle into warmed serving bowls and serve immediately with a fresh grinding of black pepper.

40 g/3 tablespoons butter

150 g/5½ oz. pancetta, cubed

1 onion, sliced

2 carrots, finely chopped

300 g/1⅔ cups thinly sliced new potatoes, unpeeled

2 tablespoons plain/all-purpose flour

600 ml/scant 2½ cups whole milk

400 ml/1⅔ cups chicken or vegetable stock

3 dried bay leaves

300 g/scant 1¼ cups sweetcorn (thawed if frozen)

3 tablespoons double/heavy cream

sea salt and freshly ground black pepper

serves 4

rocket soup with poached egg & truffle oil

25 g/1¼ tablespoons butter

2 leeks, chopped

250 g/scant 1 cup peeled and chopped potatoes

1 litre/4 cups chicken stock, plus a little extra to blend

200 g/scant 3 cups rocket/arugula

1 teaspoon white wine vinegar

4 eggs

100 ml/scant ½ cup double/heavy cream

1–2 tablespoons truffle oil

sea salt and freshly ground black pepper

serves 4

If you love truffle oil, this is a great excuse to use some of that treasured bottle. If you don't, it is perfectly fine without it. In fact, the egg makes it a substantial meal by adding a bit of protein, but it would be fine without the egg too.

Melt the butter in a large, heavy-based saucepan and add the leeks. Cover and cook over low heat for 8 minutes until soft. Add the potatoes and cook, covered, for a further 5 minutes. Pour in the stock and simmer for 15 minutes or until the potatoes are really tender. Remove from the heat and add the rocket, then let it wilt for 10 minutes.

Meanwhile, bring a deep frying pan of water to the boil, add the vinegar, then turn down to a gentle simmer. Crack the eggs around the edge of the pan so they don't touch and poach for exactly 3 minutes.

Transfer the soup to a blender and work to a purée, adding extra stock if necessary. Return to the pan, stir in the cream and season with salt and pepper.

Ladle into warmed serving bowls, topping each with a poached egg and serve immediately with a fresh grinding of black pepper and a drizzle of truffle oil.

sweet potato & coconut soup with Thai pesto

Sweet potatoes make an excellent ingredient for soups. When blended they take on a velvety, creamy texture. Here their sweetness is cut through with spicy Asian flavours in the form of a Thai-style pesto, which really brings this soup to life.

Heat the oil in a heavy-based saucepan over medium heat. Add the sweet potato and onion, partially cover with a lid and cook for 15 minutes, stirring often, until they are soft and just starting to turn golden. Increase the heat to high, add the curry paste and stir-fry with the sweet potato for 3–4 minutes so that the paste becomes fragrant. Add the stock and coconut milk and bring to the boil.

Transfer to a blender and purée until smooth. Return the blended soup to a clean saucepan.

To make the pesto, put all of the ingredients in a blender and work to a paste, occasionally scraping down the sides of the bowl.

Gently reheat the soup, then ladle into warmed serving bowls. Serve immediately, topped with a generous spoonful of Thai pesto.

1 tablespoon light olive oil

500 g/3⅓ cups peeled and cubed sweet potato

1 red onion, chopped

1 tablespoon Thai red curry paste

500 ml/2 cups vegetable stock

500 ml/2 cups coconut milk

Thai pesto

100 g/⅔ cup unsalted peanuts, lightly toasted (see page 10)

2 garlic cloves, chopped

2 teaspoons finely grated fresh ginger

2 fresh green chillies/chiles, deseeded and chopped

1 small bunch of fresh coriander/cilantro

1 large handful of fresh mint leaves

1 large handful of fresh basil leaves

2 tablespoons light soy sauce or Thai fish sauce

2 tablespoons freshly squeezed lime juice

1 tablespoon soft light brown sugar

serves 4

peppery watercress & pea soup with Gorgonzola

1 small bunch of watercress

50 g/3½ tablespoons butter

1 onion, chopped

1 celery stalk, chopped

100 g/1⅓ cups rocket /arugula

½ teaspoon cracked black pepper

300 g/2 cups peas (frozen or freshly shelled)

1.5 litres/6 cups vegetable stock

100 g/3½ oz. Gorgonzola (optional)

serves 4

Despite taking no time at all to prepare, there is something about watercress soup that seems very refined. Its mustardy bite sits nicely with the intensely flavoured Gorgonzola.

Pick over the watercress to remove any discoloured leaves. Cut off and discard about 5 cm/2 inches from the bottom of the stems. Roughly chop the leaves and remaining stems and set aside.

Melt the butter in a large heavy-based saucepan over high heat. Add the onion and celery and cook for 2–3 minutes, until soft. Add the watercress, rocket and pepper and stir-fry for a couple of minutes until the greens wilt in the hot pan. Add the peas and stock and bring to the boil. Reduce the heat and simmer for 10 minutes, until all the vegetables are very soft.

Transfer the soup to a blender and work to a purée. Pass through a sieve/strainer into a clean saucepan and gently reheat.

Cut the Gorgonzola into 4 pieces (if using) and put 1 in the bottom of each warmed serving bowl. Ladle the hot soup over the top and serve immediately.

eggs

caramelized chicory with black forest ham & poached eggs

Chicory works so well with the sweet, smoky flavours of the ham in this recipe. The chilli and lemon in the dressing wake up all the flavours. If you make this once you'll be addicted.

Preheat the oven to low.

To make the dressing, put the garlic, chilli/chile and vinegar in a bowl and whisk in the olive oil and lemon zest and juice.

Melt the butter in a large frying pan over low heat and add the chicory, cut side down. Season with salt and pepper, cover with a lid and leave to cook gently for 5–6 minutes. Remove the lid, turn up the heat and continue to cook for 5 minutes, until golden. Turn the chicory halves over and cook for 3–4 minutes to caramelize the other side. Transfer to the oven to keep warm.

Bring a deep frying pan of water to the boil, add the vinegar, then turn down to a gentle simmer. Crack the eggs around the edge of the pan so they don't touch and poach for exactly 3 minutes.

Divide the rocket/arugula between serving plates, top with 2 chicory halves and drape the Black Forest ham on top. Season with salt and pepper to taste. Put the poached eggs on top of the ham and scatter over some Parmesan shavings. Drizzle with a little dressing and serve immediately.

1 small garlic clove, finely chopped

1 fresh red chilli/chile, finely chopped

1 tablespoon red wine vinegar

2 tablespoons extra virgin olive oil

finely grated zest and juice of ½ lemon

25 g/1¼ tablespoons butter

4 chicory heads, halved lengthways

1 teaspoon white wine vinegar

4 eggs

100 g/1¼ cups rocket/arugula

8 slices of Black Forest ham

25 g/1½ cup shaved Parmesan

sea salt and freshly ground black pepper

serves 4

smoked salmon omelette

75 g/2¾ oz. smoked salmon, cut into thin strips

1 tablespoon milk

3 eggs

2 teaspoons unsalted butter

2 tablespoons crème fraîche or sour cream

1 tablespoon chopped fresh dill

sea salt and freshly ground black pepper

serves 1

It is important to start folding the omelette while it is still slightly liquid in the centre to avoid it overcooking on the bottom.

Put half the smoked salmon in a bowl, add the milk and let stand for 15 minutes.

Beat the eggs briefly in a mixing bowl. Season with salt and pepper, then stir in the milk and smoked salmon.

Heat the butter in large, non-stick frying pan. When the butter starts to foam, pour in the egg mixture and cook over medium-high heat, drawing the mixture from the sides to the centre as it sets. Let the liquid flow and fill the space at the sides.

After a short time, the omelette will be cooked but still creamy in the centre. Top the omelette with the crème fraîche and sprinkle with chopped dill and the remaining smoked salmon.

Fold over a third of the omelette to the centre, then fold over the remaining third, slide onto a warmed plate and serve immediately.

tortilla with potatoes, & roasted pimentos

The secret of a good tortilla is to soften the potatoes in lots of olive oil and then add them to the eggs and back into the pan, not the other way around. If you pour the eggs directly over the potatoes in the pan, they will not coat the potatoes evenly and you will get air bubbles.

Preheat the grill/broiler to medium-high.

Heat 4 tablespoons of the oil in a large, non-stick frying pan over medium heat, then add the potatoes, chillies/chiles, onion and salt. Reduce the heat to low and cover with a lid. Cook for 15 minutes, stirring occasionally, until soft.

Beat the eggs in a large mixing bowl. Transfer the cooked ingredients from the frying pan to the beaten eggs and stir. Add the roasted pimentos.

Heat the remaining oil in the frying pan over medium heat. Pour the egg mixture into the pan. Cook for 4–5 minutes until the base is golden – loosen the sides and lift up to check.

Slide the tortilla under the preheated grill/broiler and grill/broil for 3–4 minutes, or until golden on top. Check that the egg is set, then cut into wedges and serve immediately

6 tablespoons olive oil

600 g/3½ cups peeled and thinly sliced potatoes

2 fresh red chillies/chiles, thinly sliced

1 onion, thinly sliced

½ teaspoon sea salt

8 eggs

125 g/⅔ cup marinated roasted pimentos or marinated red bell peppers, drained and sliced

serves 6

deep-fried eggs with rice & oyster sauce

150 g/²⁄₃ cup jasmine or long-grain rice, washed

150 ml/²⁄₃ cup groundnut oil

4 eggs

2 garlic cloves, peeled and crushed

4 spring onions/scallions, sliced

1 teaspoon sesame oil

1 tablespoon light soy sauce

a pinch of white pepper

2 tablespoons oyster sauce

2 fresh red chillies/chiles, deseeded and finely chopped

a handful of fresh coriander/cilantro leaves

serves 2

These eggs are delicious with their frazzled whites and molten yolks. The spicy stir-fried rice makes this a satisfying dish that is packed with flavour and only takes minutes to prepare.

Cook the rice according to the package instructions. Drain, rinse, and set aside until needed.

Heat the groundnut oil in a wok or large saucepan over high heat – throw in a cube of bread and if it browns in 10 seconds, the oil is hot enough. Crack 2 of the eggs into a dish, then gently slide them into the wok. It will hiss and splutter, so stand back for a couple of seconds. Cook for 1–2 minutes until the whites are set but the yolks still oozy, then remove from the pan with a slotted spoon. Cook the remaining eggs in the same way and set aside until needed.

Pour away all but 1 tablespoon of the groundnut oil (you can bottle it and use it again once cool) and add the garlic. Cook until it is starting to colour, then add the cooked rice and half the spring onions/scallions. Stir-fry briskly, then add the sesame oil, soy sauce and white pepper. Give it a good stir, then transfer to 2 bowls. Put a portion of egg on each mound of rice, drizzle with oyster sauce and sprinkle over the chillies, remaining spring onions/scallions and the coriander/cilantro leaves.

field mushroom tortilla

This robust tortilla is packed full of goodness. It is so simple to prepare and makes a nutritious meal for all the family to enjoy.

Preheat the grill/broiler to medium-high.

Heat the butter and oil in a large, non-stick frying pan over medium heat, add the potatoes and brown on all sides. Transfer to a plate, then cook the mushrooms on both sides for 5 minutes, adding a little more butter or oil if necessary. Transfer to another plate and return the potatoes to the pan. Add the garlic, and then the mushrooms and spinach.

Beat the eggs and milk in a large mixing bowl. Season with salt and pepper and pour into the pan. Cook for 4–5 minutes until the base is golden – loosen the sides and lift up to check.

Slide the tortilla under the preheated grill/broiler and grill/broil for 3–4 minutes, or until golden on top. Check that the egg is set, then cut into wedges and serve immediately.

20 g/1½ cups butter

2 tablespoons olive oil

3 cooked potatoes, diced

200 g/7 oz. large flat field mushrooms

1 garlic clove, crushed

125 g/scant 2 cups young spinach

4 eggs

100 ml/scant ½ cup milk

sea salt and freshly ground black pepper

serves 4–6

spinach & pancetta frittata

1 tablespoon extra virgin olive or sunflower oil

125 g/4$\frac{1}{2}$ oz. smoked pancetta or smoked bacon, cut into cubes

4 spring onions/scallions, chopped

1 garlic clove, finely chopped

175 g/2$\frac{1}{2}$ cups baby spinach

6 eggs

sea salt and freshly ground black pepper

serves 4

Baby spinach is essential for this recipe because the leaves wilt and soften quickly, so you needn't remove the stalks or chop the leaves. The pancetta adds a special depth of flavour.

Preheat the grill/broiler to medium-high.

Heat the oil in a large, non-stick frying pan over medium heat. Add the pancetta and cook for 3–4 minutes to brown on all sides.

Add the spring onions/scallions, garlic and spinach and stir-fry for 3–4 minutes or until the spinach has wilted and the onions are soft.

Beat the eggs in a large mixing bowl. Season with salt and pepper and pour into the pan. Quickly mix with the other ingredients and cook for 8–10 minutes over low heat until the base is golden – loosen the sides and lift up to check.

Slide the tortilla under the preheated grill/broiler and grill/broil for 3–4 minutes, or until golden on top. Check that the egg is set, then cut into wedges and serve immediately.

Taleggio & potato tortilla with red pepper tapenade

Thanks to the creamy Taleggio cheese, this tortilla packs a super-rich taste punch and makes a perfect quick meal for four.

Preheat the oven to 220°C (425°F) Gas 7.

To make the tapenade, put a baking sheet in the oven for a few minutes to heat. Put the red pepper on the baking sheet and cook in the preheated oven for about 15 minutes, turning often until the skin starts to blacken and puff up. Transfer to a clean plastic bag and let cool. When the pepper is cool enough to handle, peel off the skin, roughly tear or chop the flesh and put it in a food processor. Add the garlic, pine nuts and 2 tablespoons of the oil and blend to a purée. Spoon into a bowl, add the Parmesan and stir well to combine.

Heat the remaining oil in a large, non-stick frying pan over high heat. Add the potatoes and onion and cook for 1 minute. Add the stock and cook for about 10 minutes, or until the potatoes start to soften, the stock has evaporated and the vegetables start to sizzle. Stir in the parsley and add the cheese.

Preheat the grill/broiler to medium-high.

Beat the eggs in a large mixing bowl. Season with salt and pepper and pour into the pan. Cook for 2–3 minutes until they start to puff up around the edges and the base is golden – loosen the sides and lift up to check.

Slide the tortilla under the preheated grill/broiler and grill/broil for 3–4 minutes, or until golden on top.

Smear some of the tapenade onto a serving plate and slide the tortilla onto the plate. Serve immediately with the extra tapenade.

1 large red bell pepper

1 garlic clove, chopped

50 g/½ cup pine nuts, lightly toasted (see page 10)

3 tablespoons olive oil

50 g/½ cup Parmesan, finely grated

10–12 small, waxy new potatoes, thickly sliced

1 small red onion, roughly chopped

250 ml/2 cups vegetable stock

1 handful of fresh flat-leaf parsley, chopped

100 g/1 cup chopped Taleggio cheese

4 eggs

sea salt and freshly ground black pepper

serves 4

asparagus, pecorino
& prosciutto frittata

100 g/scant 1 cup asparagus, cut into short lengths

250 g/1⅓ cups frozen broad/fava beans or peas, thawed

6 eggs

75 g/¾ cup freshly grated Pecorino

3 tablespoons chopped fresh oregano

1 tablespoon chopped fresh flat-leaf parsley

2 tablespoons extra virgin olive or sunflower oil

1 medium onion, chopped

3 thin slices Parma ham, or other prosciutto

sea salt and freshly ground black pepper

serves 3–4

Pecorino is the generic name for all Italian cheeses made from sheep's milk. Pecorino Romano from Lazio, the region around Rome, is one of the best known and probably Italy's oldest cheese. It has a sharp, dry flavour and a hard texture, perfect for grating, which makes it the best choice for this recipe.

Preheat the grill/broiler to medium-high.

Bring a saucepan of water to the boil and add the asparagus. Return the water to the boil and cook for about 5–6 minutes until just tender. Drain and refresh with cold water. If using broad/fava beans, remove the waxy skins and discard.

Beat the eggs in a large mixing bowl. Season with salt and pepper and mix in two-thirds of the cheese, all the oregano, parsley, asparagus and broad/fava beans or peas.

Heat the oil in a large non-stick frying pan over medium heat, add the onion and cook for 5 minutes, or until just starting to brown. Pour the egg mixture into the pan and quickly mix with the onion. Cook for 12–15 minutes over low heat until the base is golden – loosen the sides and lift up to check.

Sprinkle with the remaining Pecorino. Tear the Parma ham slices into 2–3 pieces and arrange on top of the frittata.

Slide the frittata under a preheated grill/broiler and grill/broil for 3–4 minutes, or until the cheese is melted and golden on top. Check that the egg is set, then carefully slide the frittata onto a warmed plate and serve immediately.

hearty country-style tortilla

This is a perfect recipe for using up small quantities of leftover vegetables. Broccoli, corn or mushrooms would also work well instead of the asparagus and green beans used here.

Preheat the grill/broiler to medium-high.

Bring a saucepan of water to the boil and add the asparagus and beans. Return the water to the boil and cook for about 5–6 minutes until just tender. Drain and refresh with cold water.

Heat 2 tablespoons of the oil in large non-stick frying pan over medium heat. Add the potatoes and cook for 5 minutes. Add the onion and cook for until just tender. Add the pepper, chorizo, asparagus, beans and garlic to the potatoes and cook for 5 minutes, stirring frequently.

Beat the eggs in a large mixing bowl. Season with salt and pepper and mix in the peas and cooked vegetable mixture.

If necessary, wipe out the frying pan with paper towels, then add the remaining oil and heat until hot. Pour the egg mixture into the pan and cook for 10 minutes over low heat until the base is golden – loosen the sides and lift up to check.

Slide the tortilla under the preheated grill/broiler and grill/broil for 3–4 minutes, or until golden on top. Check that the egg is set, then cut into wedges and serve immediately.

70 g/$\frac{1}{2}$ cup asparagus spears, cut into short lengths

75 g/$\frac{1}{2}$ cup green beans, trimmed and cut into three

4 tablespoons extra virgin olive or sunflower oil

3 medium potatoes, about 325 g/ 11$\frac{1}{2}$ oz., peeled and cubed

1 onion, halved and sliced

1 red bell pepper, thinly sliced

75 g/$\frac{1}{2}$ cup sliced spicy chorizo

1 garlic clove, finely chopped

6 eggs

75 g/$\frac{1}{2}$ cup frozen peas, thawed

sea salt and freshly ground black pepper

serves 4–6

paella tortilla

A speciality of the Alicante region in Spain is a meat paella finished with an omelette topping. This delicious tortilla version uses the shellfish typical of Paella Valenciana instead of the meat.

3 tablespoons extra virgin olive or sunflower oil

1 skinless chicken breast, about 175 g/6 oz., cut into strips

1 onion, chopped

1 garlic clove, chopped

1 red bell pepper, sliced

2 tomatoes, chopped

100 g/scant ½ cup cooked short-grain Spanish rice, such as calasparra

a pinch of saffron threads, soaked in 2 tablespoons hot water

150 g/5½ oz. ready cooked mixed seafood, such as prawns/shrimp, mussels and squid

3 tablespoons frozen peas, thawed

6 eggs

sea salt and freshly ground black pepper

serves 4–6

Preheat the grill/broiler to medium-high.

Heat 2 tablespoons of the oil in a large, non-stick frying pan, add the chicken and fry until browned. Transfer to a plate.

Add the onion, garlic and red pepper and fry for 5 minutes, stirring frequently, until softened. Stir in the tomatoes, rice and saffron. Add the chicken and season with salt and pepper. Cover and cook over gentle heat for about 5 minutes then stir in the mixed seafood and the peas.

Beat the eggs in a large mixing bowl. Season with salt and pepper and mix in the paella mixture.

If necessary, wipe out the frying pan with paper towels, then add the remaining oil and heat until hot. Pour the egg mixture into the pan and cook for 10 minutes over low heat until the base is golden – loosen the sides and lift up to check.

Slide the tortilla under the preheated grill/broiler and grill/broil for 3–4 minutes, or until golden on top. Check that the egg is set, then cut into wedges and serve immediately.

Note: If ready-mixed seafood cocktail is unavailable, use 50 g/ 1¾ oz. each of shelled prawns/shrimp, shelled mussels and squid.

tortilla with artichokes & serrano ham

This tasty tortilla is topped with cured mountain ham. You can trickle a little extra virgin olive oil over the top before grilling and, for a truly extravagant touch, add a few slices of goat cheese, which melts beautifully into the top of the tortilla.

Preheat the grill/broiler to medium-high.

Heat 2 tablespoons of the oil in large non-stick frying pan over medium heat. Add the potatoes and cook for 5 minutes. Add the onion and cook for a further 10 minutes, until just tender.

Beat the eggs in a large mixing bowl. Season with salt and pepper and mix in the artichokes, thyme and about three-quarters of the ham. Add the potatoes and onion and stir gently.

Heat the remaining oil in the frying pan over medium heat. Pour the egg mixture into the pan, spreading it evenly. Cook over medium-low heat for about 6 minutes, then top with the remaining ham. Cook for a further 4–5 minutes or until the base is golden – loosen the sides and lift up to check.

Add the goat cheese, if using, and slide the tortilla under the preheated grill/broiler and grill/broil for 2–3 minutes, or until golden on top. Check that the egg is set, then cut into wedges and serve immediately.

3 tablespoons extra virgin olive or sunflower oil

350 g/2 cups peeled and cubed potatoes

1 onion, chopped

5 large eggs

400 g/2$\frac{1}{2}$ cups canned artichoke hearts in water, well drained and cut in half

2 tablespoons fresh thyme leaves

100 g/3$\frac{1}{2}$ oz. thinly sliced serrano ham, torn into strips

6–8 slices goat cheese, about 125 g/4$\frac{1}{2}$ oz. (optional)

sea salt and freshly ground black pepper

serves 3–4

spaghetti & tomato frittata

3 tablespoons extra virgin olive oil

1 onion, chopped

1 garlic clove, crushed

3 ripe plum tomatoes, chopped

1 fresh red chilli/chile, deseeded and finely chopped

2 tablespoons tomato purée/paste

150 ml/1 cup plus 2 tablespoons white wine or water

325 g/6½ cups cold cooked spaghetti

6 eggs

2 tablespoons freshly grated Parmesan

25 g/⅓ cup rocket/arugula

2 tablespoons balsamic vinegar

sea salt and freshly ground black pepper

serves 4

This is a great way to use up leftover spaghetti. I have mixed it with a fresh arrabbiata sauce made with tomatoes and fresh chillies/chiles to add a fiery flavour.

Preheat the grill/broiler to medium-high.

Heat 1 tablespoon of the oil in a saucepan over medium heat, add the onion and cook for 5 minutes until soft. Add the garlic, tomatoes and chilli/chile and cook for 3–4 minutes, stirring several times. Add the tomato purée/paste and wine or water and simmer for 5 minutes. Remove from the heat, add the spaghetti and toss gently to combine.

Beat the eggs in a large mixing bowl. Season with salt and pepper and mix in the spaghetti and sauce.

Heat the remaining oil in the frying pan. Pour the egg mixture into the pan, spreading it evenly. Cook over low heat for 10–12 minutes until the base is golden – loosen the sides and lift up to check.

Sprinkle with the Parmesan and slide the frittata under the preheated grill/broiler and grill/broil for 30–60 seconds, or until golden on top. Check that the egg is set,then carefully slide the frittata onto a warmed plate. Put the rocket/arugula leaves on top of the frittata, sprinkle with balsamic vinegar and serve immediately.

creamy eggs with goat cheese

Stirring a little creamy goat cheese into lightly scrambled eggs transforms a simple dish into a delicious light lunch. The nasturtium flowers are optional, but they do add a delightful flash of colour as well as a delicate peppery flavour.

Beat the eggs in a large mixing bowl with the cream and marjoram and season with salt and pepper. Melt the butter in a non-stick saucepan, add the eggs and stir over low heat until the eggs are beginning to set.

Stir in the goat cheese and continue to cook briefly, still stirring, until the cheese melts into the eggs. Put a piece of toast on each warmed serving plate and spoon the eggs onto the toast. Top with the nasturtium flowers and serve immediately.

12 eggs

100 ml/scant 1 cup single/light cream

2 tablespoons chopped fresh marjoram

50 g/3½ tablespoons butter

200 g/2 cups cubed soft goat cheese

a handful of nasturtium flowers, torn (optional)

sea salt and freshly ground black pepper

toasted walnut bread, to serve

serves 4

charred asparagus & herb frittata with smoked salmon

250 g//9 oz. (about 6) asparagus spears, trimmed

1 tablespoon extra virgin olive oil

6 eggs

4 spring onions/scallions, finely chopped

2 tablespoons chopped fresh herbs, such as tarragon, dill and mint

50 g/½ cup ricotta

15 g/1 tablespoon butter

250 g/9 oz. smoked salmon

sea salt and freshly ground black pepper

serves 4

Charring the asparagus spears on a stove-top grill pan intensifies their flavour and adds a smokiness to the frittata.

Preheat the grill/broiler to medium-high.

Mix the asparagus with the oil and a little salt and pepper. Heat a grill/griddle or frying pan over high heat. Add the asparagus and cook for 3–4 minutes, turning until evenly charred. Set aside.

Beat the eggs in a large mixing bowl. Season with salt and pepper and mix in the spring onions/scallions, herbs and ricotta.

Melt the butter in a large non-stick frying pan over medium heat, Pour the egg mixture into the pan, spreading it evenly. Arrange the asparagus spears over the top and cook for 3–4 minutes until the base is golden – loosen the sides and lift up to check.

Slide the frittata under the preheated grill/broiler and grill/broil for 30–60 seconds, or until golden on top. Check that the egg is set, then cut into wedges and serve immediately with the smoked salmon on the side.

tenderstem broccoli, shiitake & tofu omelette

This is an omelette with a distinctly Asian feel as creamy cubes of tofu replace the more traditional cheese. As a variation, you can replace the broccoli with young, tender peas and add a sprinkling of fresh coriander/cilantro.

Preheat the grill/broiler to high.

Heat the oil in a large, non-stick frying pan over high heat. Add the shallots, broccoli and mushrooms and stir-fry for 3–4 minutes, until the mushrooms are soft and the broccoli turns a bright, emerald green. Add the spinach and cook until just wilted. Add the soy sauce and stir. Arrange the cubes of tofu over the vegetables so that they are evenly spaced.

Beat the eggs in a large mixing bowl and pour into the pan. Cook over high heat for 4–5 minutes until the base has puffed up – loosen the sides and lift up to check.

Slide the omelette under the preheated grill/broiler and grill/broil until golden and firm on top. Remove from the heat, let cool a little and drizzle with the oyster sauce (if using). Sprinkle with white pepper, cut into wedges and serve immediately.

1 tablespoon light olive oil

2 shallots, sliced

1 bunch of tenderstem broccoli, chopped into small pieces

200 g/scant 2 cups shiitake mushrooms

50 g/⅔ cup baby spinach leaves

2 teaspoons light soy sauce

300 g/10½ oz. firm tofu, cubed

8 eggs

ground white pepper

oyster sauce, to serve (optional)

serves 4

pasta

penne with spicy meatballs

By using good-quality beef sausages to make the meatballs, this classic Italian dish can be on the table in minutes.

Heat the oil in a frying pan over medium heat. Add the onion and garlic and cook for 2–3 minutes, until soft and just starting to brown. Add the tomatoes, tomato purée/paste, sugar, chilli/hot pepper flakes and 125 ml/1 cup water and bring to the boil. Reduce the heat to a simmer.

Using slightly wet hands, squeeze the filling out of the sausage casings, if necessary, and shape into walnut-sized balls. Add these to the tomato sauce. Simmer the meatballs in the sauce for 5 minutes, shaking the pan often to move the meatballs around so that they cook evenly.

Bring a large saucepan of water to the boil, add plenty of salt and return to the boil. Cook the pasta according to the package instructions. Drain the pasta well and return it to the warm pan.

Season the meatball sauce with salt and pepper. Divide the pasta between warmed serving plates and top with meatballs. Serve immediately topped with finely grated Parmesan.

2 tablespoons olive oil

1 onion, chopped

2 garlic cloves, crushed

2 x 400-g/14-oz. cans chopped tomatoes

1 tablespoon tomato purée/paste

½ teaspoon caster/granulated sugar

½ teaspoon dried chilli/hot pepper flakes

400 g/14 oz. skinless beef sausages or plain beef sausages

400 g/4 cups dried penne, or other pasta shape

sea salt and freshly ground black pepper

finely grated Parmesan, to serve

serves 4

tuna tartare pasta

350 g/3½ cups dried fusilli or pasta shape of your choice

6 tablespoons extra virgin olive oil

4 garlic cloves, sliced

1–2 fresh red chillies/chiles, deseeded and chopped

grated zest and juice of 1 lemon

1 tablespoon chopped fresh thyme leaves

500 g/1 lb 2 oz. tuna steak, chopped

a handful of fresh basil leaves

sea salt and freshly ground black pepper

2 halved lemons, to serve

serves 4

'Tartare' means uncooked and, to serve fish this way, you must use very fresh, sashimi-grade tuna. If you prefer your tuna cooked, sear it on a preheated grill/griddle pan or frying pan for 1 minute on each side or until cooked to your liking.

Bring a large saucepan of water to the boil, add plenty of salt and return to the boil. Cook the pasta according to the package instructions. Drain the pasta, reserving 4 tablespoons of the cooking liquid, and return both to the pan.

Meanwhile, heat the oil in a frying pan over medium heat, add the garlic and cook for 2 minutes until soft and just starting to brown. Add the chillies/chiles, lemon zest and thyme and cook for a further minute.

Stir the hot garlic oil mixture, the lemon juice, the raw tuna, basil leaves and a little extra olive oil into the pasta. Season with salt and pepper to taste. Divide the pasta between warmed serving plates and serve immediately with half a fresh lemon for squeezing.

spaghetti with spicy garlic breadcrumbs

This is one of those pasta combinations that works with just about any of your favourite seasonings. You can easily use dried chilli/hot pepper flakes instead of fresh chillies/chiles or throw in a few chopped anchovies.

Bring a large saucepan of water to the boil, add plenty of salt and return to the boil. Cook the pasta according to the package instructions and drain.

Heat half the oil in a large frying pan over medium heat. When it is hot, add the breadcrumbs and cook for 3–4 minutes, stirring constantly until evenly browned with a nutty aroma. Remove from the pan and wipe the pan clean.

Add the remaining oil to the pan and cook the courgettes/zucchini for 5 minutes over high heat, turning often, until golden and starting to look crispy. Add the garlic and chillies/chiles and cook for 4–5 minutes, stirring often.

Add the cooked pasta and breadcrumbs to the pan and toss to combine. Divide the pasta between warmed serving plates and serve immediately, topped with finely grated Parmesan.

400 g/14 oz. spaghetti, or similar pasta

90 ml/⅓ cup light olive oil

100 g/2 cups fresh breadcrumbs

8 small or baby courgettes/zucchini, cut into strips

2 garlic cloves, grated

2 small fresh red chillies/chiles, deseeded and chopped

finely grated Parmesan, to serve

serves 4

pappardelle with roast fennel, tomato & olives

65 ml/4 tablespoons extra virgin olive oil

4 tomatoes, halved

2 red onions, cut into wedges

4 small courgettes/zucchini, thickly sliced

2 small fennel bulbs, thickly sliced

2 garlic cloves, thickly sliced

1 teaspoon smoked paprika (pimentón)

50 g/scant ⅓ cup small black olives

400 g/14 oz. fresh pappardelle pasta

30 g/2 tablespoons butter

salt and freshly ground black pepper

grated Manchego, to serve

serves 4

This technique of roasting vegetables in the oven makes easy work of a pasta sauce. The vegetables soften and sweeten while they cook. If you can't find pappardelle, simply buy fresh lasagne sheets and cut them into 2-cm/¾-inch strips.

Preheat the oven to 220°C (425°F) Gas 7.

Put the olive oil in a roasting pan and place in the oven for 5 minutes to heat up.

Add all of the vegetables and the garlic to the roasting pan and sprinkle over the paprika. Season with salt and pepper to taste. Roast in the preheated oven for about 20 minutes, giving the pan a shake after 15 minutes. Remove from the oven and stir in the olives. Cover and let sit while you cook the pasta.

Bring a large saucepan of water to the boil, add plenty of salt and return to the boil. Cook the pasta according to the package instructions. Drain the pasta and return to the pan. Add the butter and toss to coat then mix in the roasted vegetables.

Arrange the pasta on a warmed serving platter and serve immediately, topped with grated Manchego.

herbed tagliatelle
with seafood skewers

A lovely, summery dish to make the most of fragrant garden herbs. Serving the prawns/shrimp on skewers adds a sense of occasion, but you can always cook them loose and add to the pasta just before serving if you prefer.

Put 4 wooden skewers in a bowl of water to soak.

Bring a large saucepan of water to the boil, add plenty of salt and return to the boil. Cook the pasta of your choice according to the package instructions.

Meanwhile, put the prawns/shrimp into a bowl and add the garlic, dried chillies/chiles, 1 tablespoon of the olive oil, and salt and pepper to taste. Mix well, then thread 5 prawns onto each skewer.

Preheat a grill pan/griddle or frying pan to hot. Add the prawn skewers to the hot pan and cook for 3 minutes on each side until pink and cooked through. Remove and keep warm. Add the lemon wedges to the pan and cook quickly for 30 seconds on each side.

Drain the pasta and return it to the warm pan. Add the remaining oil, rosemary, parsley, chives and rocket/arugula, season with salt and pepper to taste and toss to combine.

Divide the pasta between warmed serving bowls and serve immediately, topped with a prawn skewer and a lemon wedge.

350 g/12 oz. dried pasta, such as tagliatelle, linguine or fettuccine

20 uncooked tiger prawns/shrimp, peeled, with tails on

2 garlic cloves, crushed

½ teaspoon crushed dried chillies/chiles

4 tablespoons olive oil

1 lemon, cut into wedges

1 teaspoon chopped fresh rosemary

2 tablespoons chopped fresh flat-leaf parsley

1 tablespoon chopped fresh chives

a handful of rocket/arugula

sea salt and freshly ground black pepper

serves 4

tagliatelle with broccoli, anchovy & Parmesan

175 g/6 oz. dried tagliatelle

300 g/2 cups broccoli florets

1 tablespoon olive oil

2 garlic cloves, crushed

½ teaspoon dried chilli/hot pepper flakes

3 anchovy fillets, roughly chopped

100 g/scant ½ cup crème fraîche/sour cream

sea salt and freshly ground black pepper

finely grated Parmesan, to serve

serves 2

You can save time and washing up here by cooking the broccoli in the same pan as the pasta. If it's in season, you can use purple sprouting broccoli to make this dish extra colourful.

Bring a large saucepan of water to the boil, add plenty of salt and return to the boil. Cook the pasta of your choice according to the package instructions. Add the broccoli to the pasta 3–4 minutes before the end of cooking. Drain the pasta and broccoli well and reserve a little of the cooking water.

Heat the oil in a saucepan over low heat. Add the garlic, dried chilli/hot pepper flakes and anchovies and cook for about 2 minutes. Add the crème fraîche, season with a little pepper and bring to the boil. Return the cooked broccoli and pasta to the pan, adding a little of the reserved pasta cooking water to thin the sauce, if necessary. Season with salt and pepper to taste.

Divide the pasta between warmed serving bowls and serve immediately, topped with finely grated Parmesan.

pasta with fresh tomato

This sauce is best made as soon as the new season's tomatoes arrive in the shops, especially the vine-ripened varieties. If you don't have a gas stove, then simply plunge the tomatoes into boiling water for 1 minute, drain, refresh and peel the skin.

Holding each tomato with kitchen tongs or a skewer, char them over a gas flame until the skins blister and start to shrivel. Peel off the skins, chop the flesh and put into a bowl. Add the oil, chillies/chiles, garlic, basil, sugar, salt and pepper and leave to infuse while you cook the pasta (or longer if possible).

Bring a large saucepan of water to the boil, add plenty of salt and return to the boil. Cook the pasta of your choice according to the package instructions. Drain the pasta and then stir in the fresh tomato sauce.

Divide the pasta between warmed serving bowls and serve immediately, topped with finely grated Pecorino or Parmesan.

1 kg/2 lb 4 oz. ripe tomatoes

6 tablespoons extra virgin olive oil

2 fresh red chillies/chiles, deseeded and chopped

2 garlic cloves, crushed

a bunch of fresh basil, chopped

1 teaspoon caster/granulated sugar

350 g/12 oz. dried spaghetti

sea salt and freshly ground black pepper

finely grated Pecorino or Parmesan, to serve

serves 4

pasta primavera with lemony breadcrumbs

4 tablespoons light olive oil

100 g/2 cups fresh white breadcrumbs

1 tablespoon finely grated lemon zest

1 tablespoon fresh thyme leaves

50 g/½ cup finely grated Parmesan

150 g/1 cup peas
(frozen or freshly shelled)

100 g/⅔ cup green beans

1 bunch of baby asparagus, sliced

2 small courgettes/zucchini,
cut into strips

2 garlic cloves, chopped

2 ripe tomatoes, skinned, deseeded
and chopped

400 g/14 oz. spaghetti or tagliatelle

sea salt and freshly ground
black pepper

serves 4

This light Italian pasta dish can be made using just about any crisp, green vegetables you find at farmers' markets, such as green beans, peas and young courgettes/zucchini.

Heat half the oil in a frying pan over medium heat. Add the breadcrumbs, lemon zest and thyme and cook for 4–5 minutes, stirring constantly, shaking the pan so that the breadcrumbs turn an even, golden colour. Add 1 tablespoon of the Parmesan and stir to combine. Remove from the pan and set aside until needed.

Bring a large saucepan of water to the boil and add the peas, beans, asparagus and courgettes/zucchini. Return the water to the boil, then cook for 2 minutes until tender and drain well.

Heat the remaining oil in a large frying pan over high heat, add the garlic and cook for just a few seconds to flavour the oil. Add the tomatoes and cook for 1 minute until softened. Return the blanched vegetables to the pan with the tomatoes, cook for 1–2 minutes and cover to keep warm.

Bring a large saucepan of water to the boil, add plenty of salt and return to the boil. Cook the pasta of your choice according to the package instructions. Drain the pasta and return it to the warm pan. Add the vegetable and tomato mixture and half the breadcrumbs and stir to combine. Season with salt and pepper to taste.

Divide the pasta between warmed serving plates, sprinkle with the remaining breadcrumbs and serve immediately, topped with the rest of the Parmesan.

tagliatelle with peas & goat cheese pesto

Crumbly goat cheese works very well in pesto, adding a slightly creamy edge to it. Roughly crumble it in so you get pockets of the molten cheese tucked in amongst your tangle of tagliatelle.

To make the pesto, put the garlic, chillies/chiles, basil and a large pinch of salt in a food processor and process until roughly chopped.

Put the pine nuts in a dry frying pan and toast over low heat for a few minutes, shaking the pan, until they are golden all over. Add the pine nuts to the mixture in the food processor and process again until coarsely chopped. Add half the olive oil and process again. Add the remaining oil, crumble in the goat cheese and stir. Season with salt and pepper to taste.

Bring a large saucepan of water to the boil, add plenty of salt and return to the boil. Cook the pasta of your choice according to the package instructions. Drain the pasta and return it to the warm pan.

Bring a small saucepan of water to the boil and add the peas. Return the water to the boil, then cook for 4–5 minutes if fresh or 3 minutes if frozen, until tender, and drain well.

Add 2–3 generous tablespoonfuls of pesto and the peas to the tagliatelle and toss to combine, then add the remaining pesto, making sure all the pasta is thoroughly coated. Divide the pasta between warmed serving bowls and serve immediately, topped with fresh basil leaves and finely grated Parmesan.

1 small garlic clove

2 fresh green chillies/chiles, deseeded

40 g/½ cup fresh basil leaves, plus extra to serve

25 g/¼ cup pine nuts

100 ml/scant ½ cup extra virgin olive oil

100 g/1 cup goat cheese

250 g/1⅔ cup fresh or frozen peas, defrosted

400 g/14 oz. tagliatelle

finely grated Parmesan, to serve

sea salt and freshly ground black pepper

serves 4

linguine with clams, tarragon & cherry tomatoes

750 g/1 lb 2 oz. clams, cleaned and scrubbed

150 ml/scant ⅔ cup dry white wine or vermouth

350 g/12 oz. linguine

100 ml/scant ½ cup extra virgin olive oil

2 garlic cloves, peeled and thinly sliced

¼ teaspoon dried chilli/hot pepper flakes

250 g/2¼ cups halved cherry tomatoes

3 fresh tarragon sprigs, finely chopped

freshly ground black pepper

serves 4

The cherry tomatoes and tarragon work beautifully with the clams to make this simple dish satisfying and delicious. If you can't get fresh clams, used canned ones or mussels instead.

Discard any clams that do not shut when tapped sharply. Pour the white wine into a large saucepan and bring to the boil over high heat, then add the clams. Cover tightly with a lid for a couple of minutes, then stir so the unopened clams fall to the bottom. Replace the lid and cook for a further 2 minutes. By this time the clams should be open; discard any that remain closed. Transfer the remainder to a bowl with all the cooking liquid.

Bring a large saucepan of water to the boil, add plenty of salt and return to the boil. Cook the pasta according to the package instructions and drain.

Heat half the olive oil in a large saucepan, then add the garlic, chilli/hot pepper flakes and cherry tomatoes. Cook over medium heat for a few minutes until the tomatoes burst and soften. Spoon in the cooked clams and strain in 200 ml/¾ cup of the cooking liquid. Cook over high heat until the liquid boils.

Add the cooked linguine to the pan with the tarragon, the remaining olive oil and lots of pepper. Divide the pasta between warmed serving bowls and serve immediately.

linguine with tomatoes, red endive & black olives

This pasta recipe involves the Italian technique of gently blanching the garlic in warm oil so that it softens and imparts its flavour without dominating the other fresh ingredients. The bitter red endive leaves offset the fruity sweetness of the tomatoes.

Heat the oil in a large frying pan over medium heat, add the garlic and cook for a couple of minutes until soft. Add the tomatoes to the pan and cook for 2–3 minutes so that they are just soft and starting to break up. Remove from the heat, stir through the endive leaves and olives and season with salt and pepper. Set aside while cooking the pasta.

Bring a large saucepan of water to the boil, add plenty of salt and return to the boil. Cook the pasta according to the package instructions. Add the tomato sauce and half of the Parmesan and toss to combine.

Divide the pasta between warmed serving bowls and serve immediately, topped with the remaining Parmesan.

65 ml/4 tablespoons olive oil

4 garlic cloves, chopped

6 medium tomatoes of different varieties and colours, roughly chopped

1 red Belgian endive (chicory), leaves torn

1 handful of small black olives

400 g/14 oz. linguine

50 g/½ cup finely grated Parmesan

sea salt and freshly ground black pepper

serves 4

pappardelle with mushrooms, chestnuts & chives

1 tablespoon olive oil

15 g/1 tablespoon butter

2 garlic cloves, chopped

400 g/4 cups sliced portobello or field mushrooms

200 g/1 cup ready-roasted chestnuts (optional)

2 fresh thyme sprigs

125 ml/½ cup dry white wine

250 ml/1 cup single/light cream

1 bunch of chives, chopped

50 g/½ cup finely grated Pecorino, plus extra to serve

400 g/14 oz. pappardelle, tagliatelle or any other ribbon pasta

sea salt and freshly ground black pepper

serves 4

Chestnuts aren't always easy to find, but if you can get your hands on some, they really do make a wonderful addition to this hearty pasta dish.

Heat the oil and butter in a frying pan over high heat until the butter sizzles. Add the garlic and cook for 1 minute, making sure it doesn't burn. Add the mushrooms, chestnuts and thyme, reduce the heat to medium and partially cover with a lid. Cook for 10 minutes, stirring often. Add the wine to the pan and simmer until the liquid is reduced by half. Add the cream, reduce the heat and cook for 15 minutes, until the mixture thickens. Add the chives and half of the Pecorino and stir to combine. Season to taste with salt and pepper. Cover with foil to keep warm.

Meanwhile, bring a large saucepan of water to the boil, add plenty of salt and return to the boil. Cook the pasta according to the package instructions. Drain well and return to the warm pan. Add the mushroom sauce and gently toss to combine. Divide the pasta between warmed serving bowls and serve immediately topped with the remaining Pecorino.

pasta with melted ricotta & herby Parmesan sauce

This pasta is fast and fresh, with the ricotta melting into the hot pasta and coating it like a creamy sauce. The pine nuts give it crunch, while the herbs lend a fresh, scented flavour.

Bring a large saucepan of water to the boil, add plenty of salt and return to the boil. Cook the pasta of your choice according to the package instructions.

Meanwhile, heat the oil in a frying pan, add the pine nuts and fry gently until golden. Set aside.

Drain the cooked pasta, reserving 4 tablespoons of the cooking liquid, and return both to the pan. Add the pine nuts and their oil, the herbs, ricotta, half the Parmesan and plenty of pepper. Stir until evenly coated.

Divide the pasta between warmed serving bowls and serve immediately, topped the remaining Parmesan.

350 g/3½ cups dried penne or other pasta

6 tablespoons extra virgin olive oil

100 g/1 cup pine nuts

125 g/scant 2 cups chopped rocket/arugula

2 tablespoons chopped fresh flat-leaf parsley

2 tablespoons chopped fresh basil

250 g/1 cup plus 2 tablespoons ricotta, mashed

50 g/½ cup finely grated Parmesan

sea salt and freshly ground black pepper

serves 4

gnocchetti pasta with smoky Spanish-style sauce

200 g/7 oz. large raw prawns/shrimp, peeled and deveined

1 tablespoon red wine vinegar

2 tablespoons olive oil

1 red onion, chopped

1 green bell pepper, thinly sliced

100 g/3½ oz. chorizo sausage, finely chopped

½ teaspoon smoked paprika (pimentón)

1 x 400-g/14-oz. can chopped tomatoes

300 g/3 cups dried gnocchetti or any other pasta shape, such as fusilli or penne

a handful of fresh mint leaves, chopped

a handful of fresh flat-leaf parsley leaves, roughly chopped

sea salt and freshly ground black pepper

lemon wedges, to serve

serves 4

This lovely Spanish-style pasta dish combines fresh prawns/shrimp and herbs with the warm smoky flavours of chorizo and paprika.

Put the prawns/shrimp in a bowl with the vinegar and 1 tablespoon of the olive oil. Season with a little salt and pepper and set aside.

Heat the remaining olive oil in a heavy-based saucepan over high heat. Add the onion, green pepper and chorizo and cook for 4–5 minutes, until soft. Add the paprika and cook for 1 minute, stirring to combine. Add the tomatoes and 125 ml/½ cup water and bring to the boil. Cook for 5 minutes, until the sauce has thickened slightly. Set aside while you cook the pasta.

Bring a large saucepan of water to the boil, add plenty of salt and return to the boil. Cook the pasta according to the package instructions. Drain well and return to the warm pan. Add the tomato sauce and keep warm over very low heat.

Heat a non-stick frying pan to hot. Add the prawns/shrimp to the hot pan and cook for 2 minutes on each side until pink and cooked through. Stir the prawns into the pasta and season to taste. Divide the pasta between warmed serving bowls and scatter over the mint and parsley. Serve immediately with lemon wedges for squeezing.

stir-fries

stir-fried beef noodles with curry paste

This stir-fry has its origins in both Thai and Chinese culinary cultures. Using ready-made Thai green curry paste means you will have this delicious dish on the table in minutes.

Cook the noodles according to the package instructions. Drain, rinse, and set aside until needed.

Heat the oil in a wok or frying pan until hot, add the garlic and fry until golden brown. Add the Thai green curry paste, stir well and fry until fragrant.

Stirring once after each addition, add the beef, drained noodles, soy sauce, fish sauce, sugar, beansprouts, broccoli and carrot and stir-fry over high heat for 2–3 minutes.

Mix well and divide the stir-fry between warmed serving bowls and serve immediately, topped with torn coriander/cilantro leaves.

4 nests of egg noodles

2 tablespoons peanut or sunflower oil

4 small garlic cloves, finely chopped

1 tablespoon good-quality Thai green curry paste

500 g/1 lb 2 oz. beef, thinly sliced

1 tablespoon dark soy sauce

3 tablespoons Thai fish sauce

2 teaspoons sugar

100 g/1 cup beansprouts, rinsed, drained and trimmed

100 g/²⁄₃ cup broccoli florets

1 carrot, cut into fine matchsticks

a handful of fresh coriander/cilantro leaves, to serve

serves 4

Buddha's delight

½ teaspoon Chinese five-spice powder

250 g/9 oz. firm tofu, cut into
2-cm/¾-in. cubes

2 tablespoons vegetable oil

3 garlic cloves, crushed

200 g/1¼ cups small broccoli florets

200 g/2 cups halved miniature or
baby pak-choi

200 g/2 cups mangetout/snow peas

1 large carrot, cut into strips

1 red bell pepper, cut into strips

85 g/½ cup canned water chestnuts,
drained and sliced

85 g/½ cup canned sliced bamboo
shoots, drained and rinsed

cooked rice or noodles, to serve

sauce

2 tablespoons oyster sauce

2 tablespoons light soy sauce

125 ml/½ cup vegetable stock

1 tablespoon cornflour/cornstarch,
combined with 2 tablespoons
cold water

serves 4

This is a hearty and flavoursome vegetarian dish traditionally eaten on the first day of Chinese New Year – Buddhists believe that meat should not be eaten on the first five days of the year. Every Buddhist family has their own version and ingredients vary from cook to cook.

Combine all the sauce ingredients in a bowl and set aside.

Sprinkle the five-spice powder over the tofu.

Heat the oil in a wok or large frying pan until hot. Add the tofu in batches and stir-fry over high heat until golden all over. Remove the tofu from the wok and drain well on paper towels.

Add the garlic and stir-fry for 1 minute, or until golden. Add the broccoli, pak-choi, mangetout/snow peas, carrot and red pepper with a sprinkle of water and stir-fry over high heat for 2–3 minutes. Then add the water chestnuts and bamboo shoots.

Pour the sauce into the wok and bring to the boil, reduce the heat and simmer gently for 2 minutes, or until the sauce has thickened. Divide the stir-fry between warmed serving bowls of cooked rice or noodles and serve immediately.

chicken pad Thai

Spicy and satisfying, this street-food favourite packs in all the flavours of Thailand. The shrimp paste adds a distinctive savoury depth to the dish, so don't let its pungent aroma put you off.

Put the noodles in a large heatproof bowl and cover with boiling water. Soak for 20 minutes, or until softened. Drain well.

Meanwhile, put the garlic, chilli and shrimp paste, if using, in a pestle and mortar and grind until you have a rough paste. Alternatively, blitz in a food processor with a little water.

Heat the oil in a wok or large frying pan until hot. Add the paste and fry over high heat for 1 minute, or until fragrant. Season the chicken with ½ tablespoon of the fish sauce and add to the wok. Stir-fry for 4 minutes, or until just cooked through. Remove the chicken from the wok and set aside.

Heat another ½ tablespoon oil in the wok, if needed. Add the beaten eggs and leave the bottom to set, then break up with a spoon to get softly set scrambled eggs. Return the chicken to the wok with the drained noodles, beansprouts and Chinese/garlic chives. Stir well. Add the remaining fish sauce with the tamarind paste and palm sugar, then half the peanuts. Stir-fry for 2–4 minutes, or until the noodles are tender. You may need to sprinkle in a little water if the noodles look too dry. Stir in the spring onions/scallions and lime juice. Taste and add more fish sauce, if desired.

Divide the pad Thai between warmed serving plates, garnish with the chopped coriander/cilantro, chilli/chile and remaining peanuts and serve immediately with lime wedges for squeezing.

150 g/5½ oz. dried flat Thai rice noodles

2 large garlic cloves, crushed

1 large fresh red chilli/chile, deseeded and finely chopped, plus ½ chilli/chile finely chopped, to garnish

1 teaspoon shrimp paste (optional)

1 tablespoon vegetable oil, plus extra if needed

2 skinless chicken breasts, cut into 2-cm/¾-inch pieces

2 tablespoons fish sauce

2 eggs, lightly beaten

100 g/1 cup beansprouts

40 g/1½ cups Chinese/garlic chives, chopped

1 tablespoon tamarind paste

1 tablespoon palm sugar or soft light brown sugar

3 tablespoons chopped roasted peanuts

2 spring onions/scallions, thinly sliced on the diagonal

a squeeze of fresh lime juice

2 tablespoons roughly chopped coriander/cilantro leaves, to garnish

lime wedges, to serve

serves 2

Singapore noodles

250 g/9 oz. dried egg noodles

2 tablespoons peanut oil

4 shallots, finely chopped

2 garlic cloves, crushed

a 3-cm/1-inch piece of fresh ginger, peeled and grated

200 g/1 cup canned water chestnuts, rinsed, drained and coarsely chopped

200 g/7 oz. pork loin, thinly sliced

400 g/14 oz. uncooked prawns/shrimp, shelled and deveined, but tails intact

2 eggs, lightly beaten

2 tablespoons soy sauce

2 tablespoons oyster sauce

2 tablespoons Malay mild curry powder (optional)

sea salt and freshly ground black pepper

to serve

2 spring onions/scallions, finely chopped

125 ml/½ cup sweet chilli sauce

serves 2

This is one of those national dishes that is better known outside its country of origin. It is simple and versatile – you can improvise with the ingredients according to whatever you have in your storecupboard or refrigerator.

Cook the noodles according to the package instructions. Drain, rinse, and set aside until needed.

Heat the oil in a wok until hot. Add the shallots, garlic and ginger and stir-fry over high heat for 2 minutes. Add the water chestnuts, pork and prawns/shrimp and stir-fry for a further 3 minutes.

Add the beaten eggs and leave to cook for 1 minute, then add the noodles. Stir well. Season with soy sauce and oyster sauce. Turn off the heat, stir in the curry powder, if using, then add salt and pepper to taste.

Divide the stir-fry between warmed serving plates, top with the spring onions/scallions and serve immediately with a separate dish of sweet chilli sauce.

stir-fried seafood with vegetables & a balsamic dressing

Keeping a bag of mixed seafood in the freezer is a great standby for a fast dinner. It can be added frozen to rice dishes, pasta or soup – just make sure they are cooked for an extra few minutes and are piping hot.

Heat 1 tablespoon of the oil in a large frying pan or wok until hot. Add the pepper, leeks and onion and stir-fry over high heat until lightly brown. Add the cherry tomatoes and cook for a further 2 minutes. Remove the vegetables from the pan and set aside in a warm place until needed.

Heat the remaining oil in the same frying pan or wok. Add the garlic, dried chilli/hot pepper flakes and mixed seafood and stir-fry over high heat for 3–4 minutes, stirring occasionally (increase the cooking time to 7–8 minutes if the seafood is frozen).

Mix the warm vegetables with the seafood and add the balsamic vinegar at the last moment.

Divide the stir-fry between warmed serving bowls and garnish with sprigs of fresh coriander/cilantro. Serve immediately with cooked rice or noodles.

2 tablespoons olive oil

1 red bell pepper, cut into thin strips

2 leeks, trimmed and cut into strips

1 large onion, cut into thick wedges

150 g/¾ cup halved cherry tomatoes

2 garlic cloves, finely sliced

1 teaspoon dried chilli/hot pepper flakes

300 g/10½ oz. frozen mixed seafood, such as prawns/shrimp, mussels, scallops and squid rings, either defrosted or frozen

2 teaspoons balsamic vinegar

a few fresh coriander/cilantro sprigs, to garnish

serves 2

Chiang Mai chicken noodles

500 ml/2 cups peanut oil, for deep-frying

400 g/14 oz. fresh egg noodles

2 tablespoons Thai red curry paste

1 teaspoon ground turmeric

1 teaspoon ground cumin

4 boneless chicken thighs, coarsely chopped

250 ml/1 cup chicken stock

250 ml/1 cup canned coconut milk

1 tablespoon Thai fish sauce

4 spring onions/scallions, finely chopped

4 tablespoons coarsely chopped coriander/cilantro leaves

to serve

4 pink Thai shallots, thinly sliced

2 limes, halved

1 tablespoon crushed dried red chillies/chiles

serves 4

This is a popular northern Thai curried noodle soup with crisp, deep-fried wheat noodles and is very like the traditional curry noodles of neighbouring Burma.

Heat the peanut oil in a wok until hot. Add half the noodles and deep-fry for 2 minutes or until gold and crisp. Remove and drain on paper towels and set aside. Drain the oil into a heatproof container and let cool.

Cook the remaining noodles according to the package instructions. Drain, rinse, and set aside until needed.

Heat 2 tablespoons of the reserved oil in the wok until hot. Add the curry paste, turmeric and cumin and stir-fry for 2 minutes, then add the chicken and stir-fry for a further 3 minutes.

Pour in the chicken stock and bring to the boil. Reduce the heat, then add the coconut milk and fish sauce. Simmer for about 10–15 minutes, then turn off the heat and stir in the spring onions/scallions and coriander/cilantro.

Pour boiling water onto the cooled, boiled noodles to reheat; drain and divide between warmed serving bowls. Ladle the soup over each bowl and serve immediately, topped with the deep-fried noodles, shallots, limes and dried chillies/chiles.

stir-fried asparagus, tofu & peppers with lemongrass, lime leaves & honey

To lift your stir-fries out of the ordinary and into the sublime, you need to be a bit crafty with ingredients. Both lemongrass and kaffir lime leaves can be tricky to find, but they freeze well, so keep a few stored in the freezer for meals such as this.

Heat the oil in a wok or a large frying pan. Add the cashew nuts, chillies/chiles, lemongrass, lime leaves, garlic and ginger and gently stir-fry over medium/low heat for 1 minute.

Add the tofu, asparagus and red peppers and stir-fry for a further 2 minutes until they start to soften around the edges and the cashew nuts turn golden.

Pour in the tamarind paste, soy sauce and honey, along with 100 ml/⅓ cup water and turn up the heat to bring the liquid to the boil. Allow the contents of the wok to bubble up for a further 3 minutes until the vegetables are tender.

Remove the slices of ginger. Divide the stir-fry between warmed serving bowls of cooked rice or noodles and serve immediately.

1 tablespoon sunflower oil

50 g/¾ cup cashew nuts

2 large fresh red chillies/chiles, deseeded and sliced

1 lemongrass stalk (outer layer discarded), finely minced

2 kaffir lime leaves, shredded

2 garlic cloves, peeled and crushed

a 2-cm/l¾ inch piece of fresh ginger, peeled and sliced

250 g/9 oz. silken tofu, cubed

250 g/2 cups medium asparagus tips

2 red bell peppers, cut into strips

1 tablespoon tamarind paste

2 tablespoons dark soy sauce

1 tablespoon clear honey

cooked rice or noodles, to serve

serves 4

Thai baby squid with green curry paste

2 tablespoons corn or peanut oil

1 tablespoon Thai green curry paste

750 g/1 lb 10 oz. ready-cleaned baby squid

1 tablespoon freshly squeezed lime juice

grated zest of 1 lime, preferably kaffir lime

1 tablespoon Thai fish sauce

a pinch of sugar

sprigs of fresh coriander/cilantro, to serve

cooked rice or noodles, to serve

serves 4

Buy Thai red or green curry paste in larger supermarkets or Asian stores. Freeze it in ice cube trays, then keep the cubes in labelled plastic bags in the freezer – then the perfect amount is always on hand, ready for each dish.

Heat the oil in a wok until hot, add the green curry paste and stir-fry over high heat for 1 minute. Add the squid and stir-fry for 1 minute, then add the lime juice and zest, fish sauce and sugar and stir-fry for a few seconds.

Divide the stir-fry between warmed serving bowls of cooked rice or noodles and serve immediately, garnished with sprigs of fresh coriander/cilantro.

spiced mixed vegetables with cumin & fennel seeds

Transform everyday vegetables into a memorable meal with a few carefully chosen whole and ground spices. As in many Indian-influenced dishes, a spiky ginger and garlic paste forms the basis of this stir-fry. Why not make extra and keep in the fridge or freezer for another day?

Put the ginger and garlic in a pestle and mortar and grind until you have a rough paste. Alternatively, blend in a food processor with a little water.

Heat the oil in a wok or large frying pan until hot. Add the fennel and cumin seeds and stir-fry over high heat until they start to pop. Add the onion and cook for a further 3–4 minutes, or until golden. Stir in the ginger and garlic paste and stir-fry for a further 2 minutes. Spoon in the ground cumin and coriander and the chilli powder and, after a few seconds, the canned tomatoes. Cook over high heat for 1 minute, or until most of the liquid has evaporated.

Add the cauliflower and carrot into the wok with a good sprinkle of water, stir, then cover and cook for 2 minutes.

Add the green beans, season with salt and cook for a further 2–3 minutes, uncovered, until the vegetables are cooked but still a little crunchy. Taste and season with more salt if needed.

Remove from the heat and stir in the chopped coriander/cilantro. Divide the stir-fry between warmed serving bowls of cooked rice or noodles and serve immediately.

a 2-cm/³⁄₄-inch piece of fresh ginger, peeled

2 garlic cloves, crushed

1 tablespoon vegetable oil

¹⁄₂ teaspoon fennel seeds

1 teaspoon cumin seeds

1 onion, halved and sliced

¹⁄₄ teaspoon ground cumin

¹⁄₄ teaspoon ground coriander

¹⁄₂ teaspoon chilli powder

150 g/³⁄₄ cup canned chopped tomatoes

200 g/³⁄₄ cup cauliflower florets

120 g/scant 1 cup carrot, cut into strips

120 g/scant 1 cup chopped green beans

2 tablespoons chopped coriander/cilantro leaves

sea salt

cooked rice, to serve

serves 2

seafood fried rice

2 tablespoons sunflower oil

2 garlic cloves, chopped

a 3-cm/1-inch piece of fresh ginger, peeled and grated

1 fresh red chilli/chile, deseeded and chopped

350 g/12 oz. small uncooked prawns/shrimp, peeled, deveined and coarsely chopped

250 g/1¾ cups frozen peas, thawed

6 spring onions/scallions, trimmed and sliced

4 tablespoons Asian dried shrimp

2 eggs, lightly beaten

800 g/3¼ cups cooked jasmine rice (from 350 g/1½ cups uncooked rice)

3 tablespoons light soy sauce

freshly squeezed juice of ½ lemon

2 tablespoons chopped fresh coriander/cilantro

serves 4

Dried shrimp is available in most Chinese or South-east Asian stores. They add a depth of flavour, especially to seafood dishes and keep very well in the storecupboard, even after opening.

Heat the oil in a wok until hot. Add the garlic, ginger and chilli/chile and stir-fry for 30 seconds. Add the prawns/shrimp, peas, spring onions/scallions and dried shrimp and stir-fry for 2 minutes until the prawns/shrimp turn pink.

Using a spatula, push the mixture to one side. Add the beaten eggs and leave the bottom to set, then break up with a spoon to get softly set scrambled eggs. Add the rice and stir over a high heat for 2 minutes until heated through.

Stir in the soy sauce, lemon juice and coriander/cilantro. Divide the stir-fry between warmed serving bowls of cooked rice or noodles and serve immediately.

pork with chilli, Thai sweet basil & toasted coconut

Pork fillet is given a spicy boost with classic Thai flavourings and the toasted coconut finishes off this super-tasty stir-fry perfectly. If Thai sweet basil is difficult to find, simply replace with it with some fresh coriander/cilantro.

Heat a wok or large frying pan until hot. Add the coconut and dry-fry over high heat for a few minutes until golden. Remove from the wok and set aside.

Put the pork fillet between 2 large sheets of plastic wrap and hit with a rolling pin until you have flattened it to about 2 cm/¾ inch. Slice very thinly and season with salt and pepper.

Heat the oil in a wok or large frying pan until hot, then sear the pork in 2 or 3 batches over high heat, adding more oil if necessary. Remove the pork from the wok and set aside.

Add the ginger, garlic, chillies/chiles and lemongrass to the wok and stir-fry for 1 minute. Return the pork to the wok and stir for 1 minute. Add the fish sauce and chilli sauce and stir well. Cook for 2 minutes, or until the pork is completely cooked through. Remove from the heat and stir in the Thai sweet basil.

Divide the stir-fry between warmed serving bowls and serve immediately with cooked rice or noodles, garnished with the toasted coconut.

4–5 tablespoons grated fresh coconut (or desiccated, if necessary)

600 g/1 lb 5 oz. pork fillet

2 tablespoons vegetable oil

a 3-cm/1-inch piece of fresh ginger

3 garlic cloves, thinly sliced

4 whole fresh bird's-eye chillies/ chiles (optional)

1 lemongrass stalk, outer skin removed and bottom 6 cm/2½ inches bruised

1 tablespoon Thai fish sauce

2 tablespoons chilli sauce

a large handful of Thai sweet basil

sea salt and freshly ground black pepper

cooked rice or noodles, to serve

serves 4

wok-tossed jasmine rice with crabmeat & asparagus

1 tablespoon peanut oil

1 small onion, finely chopped

2 garlic cloves, crushed

1 large fresh red chilli/chile, deseeded and finely chopped

130 g/1 cup fine asparagus, chopped and tips kept separately

1 tablespoon light soy sauce, plus extra if needed

200 g/scant 1 cup canned or fresh white crabmeat, well drained

250 g/1 cup cold, cooked jasmine rice

1 tablespoon sweet chilli sauce

¼ teaspoon toasted sesame oil

2 tablespoons finely chopped chives

serves 2

This is a great way to transform storecupboard staples such as rice and canned crabmeat into a feast with the addition of a few fresh ingredients. If you are really looking to impress, then use freshly picked white crabmeat, but go easy on the flavourings, as you don't want to overwhelm the delicate sweetness of the crab.

Heat the peanut oil in a wok or large frying pan until hot. Add the onion and stir-fry over high heat for 2–3 minutes, or until softened and golden. Add the garlic and chilli/chile and cook for a further minute. Throw in the asparagus stalks and stir-fry for 2 minutes. Add the asparagus tips and 2 teaspoons of the soy sauce and stir-fry for 30 seconds. Stir in the crabmeat and cook over medium heat until heated through.

Mix in the rice, then pour in the chilli sauce, sesame oil and remaining soy sauce. Stir well until everything is thoroughly combined and the rice is heated through. Taste and add more soy sauce if needed, then stir in the chives and remove from the heat.

Divide between warmed serving bowls and serve immediately.

beef chow mein

Chow mein is a classic noodle stir-fry that should be part of every keen cook's repertoire. Treat this recipe as a basic guide to which you can add your own touches. Try varying the vegetables and replacing the beef with chicken or tofu.

Put the beef in a bowl, add all the marinade ingredients, mix well and set aside.

Cook the noodles according to the package instructions. Drain, rinse, and set aside until needed.

Combine all the sauce ingredients in a bowl and set aside.

Heat 1 tablespoon of the oil in a wok or large frying pan until hot. Add the marinated beef in 2 batches and stir-fry over high heat for 2–3 minutes, or until well sealed all over. Remove the beef from the wok and set aside.

Heat the remaining oil in the wok, then add the white parts of the spring onions/scallions and stir-fry for 30 seconds. Add the stalks of the choy sum and stir-fry for 2 minutes. Pour in the sauce and bring to the boil. Leave to bubble for 1 minute, then return the beef to the wok and stir through.

Stir the drained noodles into the wok, then cook for 1–2 minutes, or until the noodles are tender. Divide the chow mein between warmed serving bowls and serve immediately, garnished with the remaining spring onions/scallions and the chilli/chile.

300 g/10½ oz. sirloin beef or fillet, trimmed of fat and very thinly sliced

300 g/10½ oz. fresh egg noodles

1½ tablespoons peanut oil

3 spring onions/scallions, finely chopped, white and green parts kept separately

170 g/1½ cups chopped choy sum (or pak choi), stalks kept separately

1 fresh red chilli/chile, thinly sliced, to serve

marinade

1½ tablespoons dark soy sauce

½ tablespoon Chinese rice wine

½ teaspoon sugar

1 garlic clove, crushed

1 teaspoon finely grated fresh ginger

2 teaspoons cornflour/cornstarch

sauce

2 tablespoons oyster sauce

200 ml/⅔ cup chicken stock

1 tablespoon light soy sauce

1 tablespoon dark soy sauce

2 teaspoons cornflour/cornstarch

serves 2

five-spice duck with plums

2 skinless duck breasts, thinly sliced

1 teaspoon Chinese five-spice powder

2 tablespoons vegetable or peanut oil,
plus extra, if needed

1 onion, sliced

1 small aubergine/eggplant, quartered
and sliced

2 plums, stoned and cut into wedges

sea salt and freshly ground
black pepper

cooked egg noodles, to serve

sauce

3 tablespoons Chinese plum sauce

1 tablespoon rice vinegar

2 tablespoons clear honey

1 tablespoon dark soy sauce, plus
extra if needed

serves 2–3

Classic Chinese crispy duck is given an updated twist. Fresh plums mingle with slices of succulent duck dry-rubbed with aromatic five-spice powder in this original stir-fry.

Combine all the sauce ingredients in a bowl and set aside.

Put the duck in a bowl and sprinkle over the five-spice powder and a pinch of salt and pepper. Rub into the duck.

Heat the oil in a wok or large frying pan until hot. Add the duck in batches and stir-fry over high heat until sealed all over. Remove the duck from the wok and set aside.

Add the onion to the wok, with a little more oil if necessary, and stir-fry for 2 minutes, or until softened and golden. Add the aubergine/eggplant with a good sprinkling of water and stir-fry for 2–3 minutes. Return the duck to the wok and stir well. Pour in the sauce, reduce the heat and simmer for 3–4 minutes, covered, until the aubergine/eggplant is just tender.

Remove the lid, then stir in the plums and cook for 2 minutes. Add more salt or soy sauce to taste.

Divide the stir-fry between warmed serving bowls and serve immediately with cooked egg noodles.

Shanghai pork noodles

This recipe is the simplest, easiest and quickest foolproof stir-fry. A satisfying mid-week meal that will be ready in minutes.

Put the noodles into a large bowl, add boiling water to cover and let soak for 15 minutes. Drain, rinse under cold running water and drain again.

Put the shiitake mushrooms into a bowl, add 125 ml/1 cup boiling water and let soak for 10 minutes. Drain, but keep the soaking water. Remove and discard the stems and slice the caps thinly.

Put the dried shrimp into a bowl, add 125 ml/½ cup boiling water and soak for 10 minutes. Drain, but keep the soaking water.

Heat the oil in a wok until hot. Add the garlic, ginger, pork, mushrooms, shrimps, carrot, bamboo shoots and mangetout/snow peas and stir-fry over high heat for 5 minutes or until cooked through.

Add the noodles and the reserved soaking water from the mushrooms and shrimp. Season with soy sauce, salt and pepper to taste. Stir well and let the noodles soak up the juices.

Divide the noodles between warmed serving bowls and serve immediately, topped with sliced spring onions/scallions.

400 g/14 oz. dried rice vermicelli or rice stick noodles

4 dried shiitake mushrooms

2 tablespoons Asian dried shrimp

4 tablespoons peanut oil

1 garlic clove, finely crushed

a 3-m/1-inch piece of fresh ginger, peeled and grated

50 g/2 oz. pork fillet, cut into strips

1 carrot, cut into strips

50 g/½ cup canned bamboo shoots, cut into strips (or baby corn)

a large handful mangetout/snow peas, cut into strips

2 tablespoons soy sauce

sea salt and freshly ground black pepper

2 spring onions/scallions, sliced on the diagonal, to serve

serves 4

gingered chicken noodles

2 tablespoons rice wine, such as
Chinese Shaohsing or Japanese mirin

2 teaspoons cornflour/cornstarch

350 g/12 oz. skinless chicken breasts,
chopped into small chunks

175 g/6 oz. dried egg noodles

3 tablespoons peanut or sunflower oil

a 3-cm/1-inch piece of fresh ginger,
peeled and finely sliced

125 g/scant 1 cup mangetout/snow
peas, finely sliced

4 tablespoons chopped fresh
Chinese/garlic chives or chives

125 g/1 cup cashew nuts, toasted in a
dry frying pan, then chopped

sauce

100 ml/scant ½ cup chicken stock

2 tablespoons dark soy sauce

1 tablespoon lemon juice

1 tablespoon sesame oil

2 teaspoons soft brown sugar

serves 4

*Most noodle dishes take just a matter of minutes to cook – in
fact, noodles made of rice flour or mung bean starch are ready
almost instantly. Wheat-based noodles take the most time – but
even then, only about the same as regular pasta.*

Put the rice wine and cornflour/cornstarch in a bowl and mix well.
Add the chicken, stir well and set aside to marinate.

Cook the noodles according to the package instructions, then drain
and shake dry.

Put all the sauce ingredients into a small bowl and mix well.

Heat half the oil in a wok or large frying pan until hot, then add the
chicken and stir-fry over high heat for 2 minutes until golden.
Remove the chicken from the wok, set aside and wipe the wok
clean. Add the remaining oil, then the ginger and mangetout/snow
peas and fry for 1 minute. Return the chicken to the wok, then add
the noodles and sauce. Cook for 2 minutes until heated through.

Add the Chinese/garlic chives and cashew nuts and stir well. Divide
the noodles between warmed serving bowls and serve immediately.

family favourites

cheeseburger

This version of a cheeseburger is made using a good-quality cheese cut into slices rather than the processed cheese often used. You can vary the cheese – for something a little different, try Camembert or crumbled Roquefort.

Put the beef, onion, garlic, thyme and some salt and pepper in a bowl and work together with your hands until evenly mixed and slightly sticky. Divide into 4 portions and shape into patties.

Brush the patties lightly with olive oil and barbecue or grill/broil for 5 minutes on each side until lightly charred and cooked through. Top the patties with the cheese slices and set under a hot grill/ broiler for 30 seconds to melt the cheese. Keep them warm.

Toast the buns, then spread each base and top with mayonnaise. Add the lettuce leaves, cheese-topped patties, tomato and onion slices and the bun tops. Arrange the burgers on warmed serving plates and serve immediately.

750 g/ 1 lb 10 oz. beef mince/ ground beef

1 onion, finely chopped

1 garlic clove, crushed

2 teaspoons chopped fresh thyme

125 g/4½ oz. Cheddar cheese, sliced

4 burger buns, halved

4 tablespoons mayonnaise

4 large lettuce leaves

2 tomatoes, sliced

½ red onion, thinly sliced

sea salt and freshly ground black pepper

olive oil, for brushing

serves 4

seafood curry

2 tablespoons vegetable oil

1 onion, grated

3 garlic cloves, crushed

a 5-cm/2-inch piece of fresh ginger, peeled and sliced

1 mild fresh red chilli/chile, chopped

1 teaspoon turmeric

2 teaspoons curry powder

1 teaspoon ground coriander

1 teaspoon ground cumin

400 g/14 oz. cooked peeled prawns/shrimp

1 x 400-g/14-oz. can chopped tomatoes

juice of 2 limes

a bunch of chopped coriander/cilantro

sea salt and freshly ground black pepper

cooked basmati rice, to serve

serves 4

Tiger prawns/shrimp or any other large peeled prawn/shrimp are ideal for this colourful, citrus-flavoured curry.

Heat the oil in a large pan over medium heat. Add the onion, garlic, ginger and chilli/chile and cook for 5 minutes. Add the turmeric, curry powder, ground coriander and cumin and mix well. Add the prawns/shrimp and cook for 3 minutes.

Pour in the tomatoes and lime juice, season and bring to the boil. Reduce the heat and simmer for 5 minutes, then add the chopped coriander/cilantro. Divide the curry between warmed serving bowls of cooked basmati rice and serve immediately.

spicy sausage & pepper pizza

Do avoid those thick and doughy frozen pizza bases. Use the really good-quality, 'authentic', organic, stonebaked, thin and crispy bases that are now available from larger supermarkets. All of the topping ingredients can be sourced from one good deli counter. If you need a vegetarian alternative, simply substitute the sausages with marinated, chargrilled artichoke hearts.

Preheat the oven to 220°C (425°F) Gas 7.

Spread the passata over the pizza bases and randomly top with the sausages, mozzarella, jalapeño and red pepper.

Bake in the preheated oven for about 15 minutes, until the pizza bases are golden and the sausage has cooked through.

Remove the pizzas from the oven and cut into slices. Serve immediately with a green salad on the side.

125 ml/1 cup passata (Italian sieved tomatoes)

2 x 22-cm/8½-inch good-quality, thin and crispy, ready-made pizza bases

2 spicy Italian sausages, thinly sliced

2 balls of fresh mozzarella

2 tablespoons pickled jalapeño slices

1 large roasted or chargrilled red bell pepper in oil, thinly sliced

a green salad, to serve

serves 4

quick Thai chicken curry

200 g/scant 1 cup Thai jasmine or
fragrant rice

1 x 400-ml/14-oz. can of coconut milk

50 g/3 tablespoons green Thai
curry paste

1 tablespoon sunflower oil

1 chicken breast (about 400 g/14 oz.),
cut into bite-sized pieces

½ teaspoon kaffir lime leaf purée

1 teaspoon Thai fish sauce

100 g/scant 1 cup mixed fresh
vegetables of your choice (see right)

a handful of Thai sweet basil leaves

serves 2

You can add your choice of vegetables to this basic curry recipe, such as sliced mushrooms, trimmed green beans, fresh spinach, bamboo shoots or sticks of courgette/zucchini and carrot. Jasmine or fragrant rice is a delicately scented rice native to Thailand.

Cook the rice according to the package instructions.

Meanwhile, pour the coconut milk into a saucepan and gently bring it to near boiling. Remove from the heat and stir in the Thai curry paste. Set aside.

Heat the oil into a large frying pan or wok and stir-fry the chicken pieces over high heat for 2 minutes, or until golden.

Pour the warm, spiced coconut milk over the fried chicken pieces and add the kaffir lime leaf purée and fish sauce. Add any vegetables you are using at this stage. Stir and simmer gently for about 12 minutes, or until everything is cooked through.

Divide the curry between warmed serving bowls, scatter over the basil leaves and serve immediately with a bowl of rice on the side.

lamb in pita bread

The spices and flavourings used in this recipe are typical of North African cooking, and all over the region pita bread is stuffed with grilled meat, salad and yogurt.

Put the coriander and cumin seeds into a small frying pan and fry until they start to brown and release their aroma. Let cool slightly, then grind to a powder with a pestle and mortar or a spice grinder.

Heat the oil in a frying pan, add the onion, garlic and ground spices and fry gently for 5 minutes until softened but not golden. Increase the heat, add the lamb and the pinch of salt and stir-fry for 5–8 minutes until well browned. Stir in the fresh coriander/cilantro.

Meanwhile, lightly toast the pita bread and cut a long slit in the side of each one. Carefully fill each pita bread with a few salad leaves, add the minced lamb mixture, a spoonful of yogurt or tahini and sprinkle with sesame seeds. Arrange on warmed serving plates and serve immediately

2 teaspoons coriander seeds

1 teaspoon cumin seeds

2 tablespoons extra virgin olive oil

1 onion, finely chopped

2 garlic cloves, crushed

1 teaspoon ground cinnamon

$1/4$–$1/2$ teaspoon cayenne pepper

300 g/10½ oz. minced/ground lamb

a pinch of salt

2 tablespoons chopped fresh coriander/cilantro leaves

4 pita breads

a few salad leaves, such as cos lettuce and watercress

plain yogurt or tahini sauce

1 tablespoon white sesame seeds, toasted in a dry frying pan

serves 4

harissa-spiced chickpeas with halloumi & spinach

1 tablespoon olive oil

1 onion, finely chopped

1 garlic clove, crushed

1 tablespoon harissa paste (see right)

1 x 400-g/14-oz. can chickpeas, drained

1 x 400-g/14 oz. can chopped tomatoes (flavoured with garlic or mixed herbs, if available)

125 g/1 cup halloumi cheese, cubed

100 g/1¼ cups baby spinach leaves

sea salt and freshly ground black pepper

freshly squeezed juice of ½ lemon

finely grated Parmesan and crisp green salad, to serve

serves 2

Halloumi is a firm cheese that is delicious eaten when hot and melting. It has a reasonably long shelf-life before it is opened, which means you can keep a pack tucked away in the fridge. Harissa is a fiery chilli/chile paste used in North African cooking – add more if you like your food spicy.

Heat the oil in a large saucepan over medium heat and gently cook the onion and garlic until softened. Add the harissa paste, chickpeas and chopped tomatoes. Bring to the boil and let simmer for about 5 minutes.

Add the halloumi and spinach, cover and cook over a low heat for a further 5 minutes. Season with salt and pepperto taste and stir in the lemon juice. Divide between warmed serving plates and sprinkle with Parmesan. Serve immediately with a green salad on the side.

Variation: Substitute a 400-g/14-oz. can of any beans (such as borlotti, kidney or cannellini) for the chickpeas.

chunky vegetable burgers with pesto

The smoky taste of chargrilled aubergines and the basil pesto give these burgers a distinctive Mediterranean flavour. You could replace the sliced tomatoes with sun-dried tomatoes if you like.

To make the pesto, put the basil, garlic, pine nuts, oil and some salt and pepper in a food processor and work to a purée. Transfer to a bowl, stir in the Parmesan and add more salt and pepper to taste. Set aside until needed.

Cut the aubergine/eggplant into 1 cm/½ inch slices. Put the oil, vinegar, garlic, and some salt and pepper in a bowl, whisk to mix, then brush over the aubergine/eggplant slices. Arrange them on a foil-lined grill/broiler pan and grill/broil under a preheated hot grill/broiler for 3–4 minutes on each side until charred and softened.

Lightly toast the rolls and top with a slice of aubergine/eggplant. Spread with pesto, add another slice of aubergine/eggplant, then add a slice of tomato and mozzarella. Drizzle with more pesto, then top with rocket/arugula and add the tops to the rolls. Arrange the burgers on warmed serving plates and serve immediately.

1 large aubergine/eggplant, about 750 g/1 lb 10 oz.

4 tablespoons extra virgin olive oil

1 tablespoon balsamic vinegar

1 garlic clove, crushed

4 soft bread rolls, halved

2 beefsteak tomatoes, thickly sliced

200 g/7 oz. mozzarella, sliced

a handful of rocket/arugula

sea salt and freshly ground black pepper

pesto

50 g/1 cup fresh basil leaves

1 garlic clove, crushed

4 tablespoons pine nuts

7 tablespoons extra virgin olive oil

2 tablespoons freshly grated Parmesan

serves 4

Spanish sausage & butter bean tagine

1 tablespoon olive oil

1 onion, finely chopped

2 garlic cloves, crushed

75 g/2¾ oz. chorizo sausage, skin removed and cut into 1-cm/ ½-inch slices

100 ml/scant ½ cup red wine

1 x 400-g/14-oz. can chopped tomatoes

1 red onion, cut into thin petals

1 x 400-g/14-oz. can butter beans, drained

1 teaspoon dried mixed herbs

a few fresh rosemary or thyme sprigs

sea salt and freshly ground black pepper

2 tablespoons of finely grated Parmesan

warm crusty bread, to serve

serves 2

This is a cheat's version of a Spanish peasant stew called a Fabada – beans, sausage and a rich tomato and red wine sauce make a welcoming supper on a cold winter's evening. If you can't get hold of chorizo, any spicy sausage will do.

Heat the oil in a large, high-sided frying pan over medium heat. Add the chopped onion and garlic and cook for a few minutes, until soft. Add the chorizo and cook for a further 2–3 minutes.

Add the red wine and bring to the boil. Allow to bubble until the mixture is reduced by half. Add the tomatoes, red onion, butter beans, 100 ml/scant 1 cup water and the dried mixed herbs and rosemary or thyme sprigs and simmer, uncovered, for 10 minutes.

Season with salt and pepper to taste and divide between warmed serving bowls. Sprinkle with the Parmesan and serve immediately with chunks of warm crusty bread.

tuna steak with warm potato salad & salsa verde

The salsa verde that accompanies this tuna steak requires a bit of chopping, but gives the meaty fish a wonderfully intense flavour. .

First make the potato salad. Put the potatoes in a large saucepan of water and bring to the boil. Reduce the heat and cook until tender. Meanwhile, pour the olive oil into a medium bowl and add the lemon juice, mustard and chives. Whisk to form a dressing.

Drain the potatoes and refresh with cold water. When cool enough to handle, halve or quarter if necessary. Toss them in the dressing until they are thoroughly coated. Set aside.

Combine all the ingredients for the salsa verde in a small bowl and mix well. Taste and season with a little pepper if needed.

Preheat a grill pan/griddle or frying pan over high heat. Brush the tuna steaks with olive oil and season with salt and pepper. Add to the preheated pan and cook for 3 minutes on each side or until barred with brown but pink in the middle. Remove from the pan and cut into pieces.

Arrange the warm potato salad on each plate and top with the tuna. Spoon the salsa verde over the top and serve immediately with spinach leaves dressed with a drizzle of extra virgin olive oil.

4 fresh tuna steaks
(150 g/5½ oz. each)

2 tablespoons extra virgin olive oil,
plus extra to serve

sea salt and freshly ground
black pepper

a few fresh spinach leaves, to serve

for the potato salad

300 g/10½ oz. baby new potatoes,
scrubbed

100 ml/⅓ cup extra virgin olive oil

freshly squeezed juice of 1 lemon

2 teaspoons wholegrain mustard

2 teaspoons chopped fresh chives

for the salsa verde

50 g/1 cup fresh flat-leaf parsley,
chopped

2 tablespoons capers, drained, rinsed
and chopped

4 anchovy fillets, soaked in milk,
drained and finely chopped

3 garlic cloves, crushed

10 green olives, pitted and chopped

80 ml/scant ⅓ cup extra virgin olive oil

serves 4–6

pan-fried chicken with creamy beans & leeks

4 boneless chicken breasts

25 g/2 tablespoons butter

1 tablespoon extra virgin olive oil

ready-made herb butter (optional)

creamy flageolet beans with leeks

50 g/3½ tablespoons butter

2 leeks, finely chopped

1 garlic clove, crushed

2 teaspoons chopped fresh rosemary

800 g/10 cups canned flageolet beans, drained and rinsed,

300 ml/1¼ cups vegetable stock

4 tablespoons double/heavy cream

sea salt and freshly ground black pepper

to serve

watercress salad

lemon wedges

serves 4

This chicken dish makes dinner simple and quick. Serve it with a peppery watercress salad and fresh lemon wedges.

To cook the beans and leeks, melt the butter in a saucepan over medium heat, add the leeks, garlic and rosemary and cook gently for 5 minutes until soft but not golden.

Add the beans, stir once, then pour in the stock. Bring to the boil, cover and simmer for 15 minutes. Remove the lid, stir in the cream, add salt and pepper to taste, then simmer, uncovered, for a further 5 minutes until the sauce has thickened. Set aside until needed.

Season the chicken with salt and pepper. Heat the butter and oil in a frying pan and cook the chicken skin side down for 4 minutes, turn it over and cook for a further 4 minutes.

Top each chicken breast with a couple of slices of the herb butter, if using, and let rest for 2–3 minutes in a warm oven.

Divide the beans and leeks between warmed serving plates, top each with a chicken breast and serve immediately with a simple watercress salad and a lemon wedge for squeezing.

wild salmon & sorrel cakes with buttered spring greens

Wild salmon is not an inexpensive fish but it is a true seasonal treat. If it isn't available, farmed salmon will also work well in this recipe. The lemony bite of the sorrel here makes it a perfect partner for the salmon in these delicious fish cakes.

Put the bay leaves and milk in a small frying pan and bring to simmering point. Add the salmon, turn off the heat and let it poach for 5 minutes. Remove the salmon and discard the poaching liquid. When the salmon is cool enough to handle, gently flake the flesh and put it in a large bowl.

Put the potatoes in a large saucepan of water and bring to the boil. Reduce the heat and cook for 10 minutes. Drain and roughly mash them. Let cool to room temperature. Put the mashed potatoes in the bowl with the salmon and add the sorrel, egg, spring onions/scallions and 80 g/scant 2 cups of the breadcrumbs. Season well with salt and pepper. Using your hands, form the mixture into 8 large patties.

Put the remaining breadcrumbs in a bowl and gently roll the fish cakes in the crumbs to evenly coat all over. Heat the oil in a non-stick frying pan over medium heat and cook the fish cakes for 3–4 minutes on each side, until the crumbs are cooked and golden.

Cook the spring greens in a saucepan of boiling water for 5 minutes and drain. Add the butter and lemon juice to the warm pan and stir well. Return the greens to the pan, season with salt and toss to coat.

Divide the greens between warmed serving plates, top with the fish cakes and serve immediately with lemon wedges for squeezing.

2 fresh bay leaves

500 ml/2 cups whole milk

500 g/1 lb 2 oz. wild salmon

3 medium potatoes (about 600 g/
1 lb 5 oz.), quartered

6–8 large sorrel leaves, thinly sliced
or 1 teaspoon lemon thyme leaves

1 egg, lightly beaten

4 spring onions/scallions, chopped

240 g/scant 5 cups fresh breadcrumbs

65 ml/4 tablespoons light olive oil

1 bunch of spring greens, thickly sliced

2 tablespoons butter

2 tablespoons freshly squeezed
lemon juice

sea salt and freshly ground
black pepper

lemon wedges, to serve (optional)

serves 4

griddled steaks with new potatoes & Roquefort

700 g/1 lb 9 oz. new potatoes

four 250-g/9-oz. sirloin or rib-eye steaks (2 cm/³⁄₄ inch thick)

5 tablespoons good-quality extra virgin olive oil

1 garlic clove, peeled and crushed

2 tablespoons capers

finely grated zest and juice of 1 lemon

50 g/³⁄₄ cup wild rocket/arugula

75 g/³⁄₄ cup Roquefort

sea salt and freshly ground black pepper

serves 4

Cooking steaks well is all about getting the pan very hot and creating a golden crust on the meat that prevents any juices from escaping. Leave them to rest after cooking and squeeze over lemon juice (an Italian trick), which cuts through the richness of the meat.

Put the potatoes in a large saucepan of water and bring to the boil. Reduce the heat and cook for 20 minutes, or until very tender, then drain and return to the pan.

Meanwhile, preheat a grill pan/griddle or large frying pan over very high heat. Drizzle the steaks with 1 tablespoon of the olive oil and season with salt and pepper. When the pan is smoking, add the steaks. Leave them to cook on one side for 3 minutes. Turn them over and cook for a further 2–3 minutes. Prod them to check if they are done to your liking: a little give means medium and lots of give means rare. Transfer them to a plate, cover with aluminium foil and leave to rest for a few minutes.

Mix the remaining olive oil with the garlic, capers and lemon zest, season well and set aside. Lightly crush the potatoes with the back of a spoon, then fold in the rocket/arugula and the olive oil mixture. Crumble over the Roquefort and divide between warmed serving bowls. Pour the lemon juice all over the steaks and cut into strips. Top the potatoes with strips of steak, pour over any juices from the steak pan and sprinkle with freshly ground black pepper.

spinach & cheese curry

Paneer is a firm, fresh white Indian cheese. It's not that easy to find, but halloumi can be used as a substitute here, as it also works well in this recipe.

Heat the oil in a non-stick frying pan over high heat and cook the cubes of cheese for 2–3 minutes, turning often, until golden all over. Remove the cheese from the pan and set aside until needed.

Heat the butter in the pan until sizzling, add the curry paste and green chillies/chiles and stir-fry for 2 minutes. Add the spinach and coriander/cilantro and cook for 3–4 minutes, until the spinach has wilted, then stir in the cream.

Put the mixture in a food processor and blend until the sauce is thick and smooth. Return to the pan, add the cheese and cook over low heat for 2–3 minutes, to heat the cheese through.

Divide the curry between warmed serving bowls of cooked basmati rice and serve immediately with lemon wedges for squeezing.

1 tablespoon vegetable oil

250 g/2 cups paneer or halloumi, cut into 2-cm/³/₄-inch cubes

2 tablespoons butter

2 tablespoons mild Indian curry paste (Madras or balti)

2 large fresh green chillies/chiles (optional), deseeded and chopped

500 g/6½ cups spinach, roughly chopped

a handful of chopped fresh coriander/cilantro, leaves and stems

125 ml/½ cup single/light cream

cooked basmati rice

lemon wedges, to serve

serves 4

prosciutto-wrapped fish with walnut pesto & balsamic tomatoes

3 tablespoons extra virgin olive oil

24 cherry tomatoes

1 tablespoon balsamic vinegar

4 slices of prosciutto

4 white fish cutlets, of 200 g/
7 oz. each

sea salt and freshly ground
black pepper

walnut pesto

1 handful of fresh
flat-leaf parsley leaves

1 handful of mint leaves

2 handfuls of basil leaves

2 tablespoons chopped fresh dill

100 g/1 cup walnuts

1 garlic clove, crushed

175 ml/1¼ cups light olive oil

50 g/½ cup finely grated Parmesan

serves 4

This recipe uses snapper cutlet, but you can use a similar weight and cut of any firm white fish here. For the pesto we have a simple twist on the classic, replacing the traditional pine nuts with walnuts, which are combined with the most wonderfully fresh spring herbs.

To make the walnut pesto, put the herbs, walnuts, garlic and olive oil in a food processor and blend until chunky. Transfer to a bowl and stir in the Parmesan. Season to taste with salt and pepper. Cover and refrigerate until needed.

Heat 2 tablespoons of the olive oil in a non-stick frying pan over high heat and add the tomatoes. Cook for 2–3 minutes, shaking the pan. Add the balsamic vinegar and season with salt and pepper. Cover with a lid and shake the pan over high heat for 1 minute, until the tomatoes soften and start to burst.

Remove the tomatoes and wipe the pan clean. Wrap a slice of prosciutto around the centre of each fish cutlet. Add the remaining oil to the pan and cook the fish cutlets for 2–3 minutes on each side, until the prosciutto is golden and crispy.

Put 1 fish cutlet on each warmed serving plate with the balsamic tomatoes and serve immediately with a generous helping of pesto on the side.

summer vegetable skewers with homemade pesto

Full of sunshine flavours, these skewers can be served with couscous or a salad. Homemade pesto is very personal – some people like it very garlicky, others prefer lots of basil or Parmesan – so simply adjust the quantities to suit your taste.

To make the pesto, put the garlic with the basil leaves, salt, pine nuts and olive oil in a food processor and blend until smooth. Transfer to a bowl and stir in the Parmesan. Season to taste with salt and pepper. Cover and refrigerate until needed.

Put all the prepared vegetables in a bowl. Mix together the olive oil, lemon juice, garlic and salt and pour it over the vegetables. Using your hands, toss the vegetables gently in the marinade, then thread them onto skewers.

Preheat a grill pan/griddle or frying pan over high heat. Cook the skewers in the preheated pan for 2–3 minutes on each side, until the vegetables are nicely browned. Divide the skewers between warmed serving plates and serve immediately with a generous helping of pesto on the side.

2 aubergines/eggplant, cut into chunks

2 courgettes/zucchini, cut into chunks

2–3 bell peppers, cut into chunks

12–16 cherry tomatoes

4 red onions, cut into quarters

for the marinade

4 tablespoons olive oil

freshly squeezed juice of ½ a lemon

2 garlic cloves, crushed

1 teaspoon sea salt

for the pesto

3–4 garlic cloves, roughly chopped

leaves from a large bunch of fresh basil (at least 30–40 leaves)

½ teaspoon sea salt

2–3 tablespoons pine nuts

extra virgin olive oil, as required

about 60 g/⅓ cup finely grated Parmesan

serves 4–6

jerk chicken wings with avocado salsa

12 chicken wings

2 tablespoons extra virgin olive oil

1 tablespoon jerk seasoning powder or 2 tablespoons paste

freshly squeezed juice of ½ lemon

1 teaspoon salt

avocado salsa

1 large ripe avocado, roughly chopped

2 ripe tomatoes, peeled, deseeded and chopped

1 garlic clove, crushed

1 small fresh red chilli, deseeded and chopped

freshly squeezed juice of ½ lemon

2 tablespoons chopped fresh coriander/cilantro

1 tablespoon extra virgin olive oil

sea salt and freshly ground black pepper

serves 4

Jerk seasoning is Jamaica's popular spice mix, used to spark up meat, poultry and fish. The seasoning is a combination of allspice, cinnamon, chilli/chile, nutmeg, thyme and sugar and is widely available from larger supermarkets and specialist food stores.

Put the chicken wings in a ceramic dish. Mix the oil, jerk seasoning, lemon juice and salt in a bowl, pour over the wings and stir well until evenly coated. Cover and refrigerate for 15 minutes.

Meanwhile, to make the salsa, put all the ingredients into a bowl, mix well and season to taste.

Cook the chicken wings either on a barbecue or under a hot grill/broiler for 5–6 minutes each side, basting occasionally with any remaining marinade until charred and tender.

Put the wings on a warmed serving platter and serve immediately with the salsa on the side.

Note: If you don't have any jerk seasoning to hand, try another spice mix or spice paste instead. Just remember, jerk is very fiery indeed, so you need a spicy one.

desserts

roast figs with honey & marsala

These ripe, luscious figs poached in the mellow distinctive flavour of Marsala and served with creamy ricotta cheese are hard to beat. If figs aren't available, you can use ripe peaches or plums, but they will need an extra 5–10 minutes' cooking time.

Preheat the oven to 200°C (400°F) Gas 6.

Put the honey, butter, cinnamon and Marsala or dessert wine in a small saucepan. Heat gently over low heat and bring to the boil. Let it bubble for 1–2 minutes, until slightly thickened.

Using a small, sharp knife, make a 1-cm/½-inch deep, star-shaped cut in the top of each of the figs. Gently squeeze the bases with your fingers to open each fruit up like a flower.

Arrange the figs upright in an ovenproof dish so that they fit tightly and pour the wine mixture over each fig. Cook in the preheated oven for about 8–10 minutes, or until slightly charred on the tips and golden.

Divide the figs between serving plates and add a generous spoonful of ricotta to each. Spoon the deliciously syrupy juices over the top and serve immediately.

3 tablespoons lavender or Greek honey

25 g/2 tablespoons unsalted butter, melted

1 teaspoon ground cinnamon

50 ml/4 tablespoons Italian Marsala wine or sweet dessert wine

8 large, ripe figs

100 g/scant ½ cup ricotta cheese, to serve

serves 4

warm compote with peaches, apricots & blueberries

2 oranges
3 ripe peaches, sliced
8–12 apricots, halved
175 g/1¾ cups blueberries
25 g/2 tablespoons caster sugar
1 cinnamon stick
plain yogurt, to serve

serves 4

A simple fruit compote that is best served warm. You can use nectarines instead of peaches, plus whatever berries you like.

Peel 1 of the oranges, removing only the zest and not the bitter white pith. Cut the peel into thin strips and put in a shallow saucepan. Squeeze the juice from both oranges and add to the pan.

Add the fruit, sugar and cinnamon stick and heat gently until the sugar dissolves. Cover the pan and simmer gently for 4–5 minutes, until the fruits are softened.

Remove from the heat and spoon into serving bowls. Add a generous spoonful of plain yogurt to each bowl and serve warm.

classic banana split

This American classic harks back to the days when bananas were a special treat rather than an everyday fruit. I think it's the outrageous combination of three sauces and three flavours of ice cream that makes it so irresistibly delicious!

Peel the bananas and cut them in half lengthways. Arrange split -side up in boat-shaped dishes. Put 1 scoop of each flavour of ice cream down the length of each banana, between the 2 halves. Drizzle the 3 sauces generously over the top.

Spoon the whipped cream over the ice cream. Sprinkle liberally with chopped nuts and top with glacé cherries. Set the wafers in the ice cream at an angle and serve immediately.

4 large ripe bananas

4 scoops each of vanilla, chocolate and strawberry ice cream

4 tablespoons each of chocolate, toffee and raspberry sauce

to serve

250 ml/1 cup whipping cream, whipped

4 tablespoons chopped mixed nuts

12 glacé/candied cherries, halved

4 fan wafers

serves 4

apple & blueberry tarts

375 g/13 oz. sheet ready-rolled
puff pastry, defrosted if frozen,
cut into 4 squares each about
12 cm/5 inches square

2 tablespoons caster/
granulated sugar

1 vanilla bean, cut in half lengthways

3 sweet dessert apples (such as Red
Delicious or Braeburn), each cored and
cut into 10–12 thin wedges

1 punnet/basket blueberries (about
150 g/1½ cups)

double/heavy cream, to serve

serves 4

*These are a cheat's delight – so simple and quick to make and
deliciously fresh-tasting. Any leftover tarts can be served cold and
enjoyed with coffee the next day. Just dust them with some icing
sugar and eat them as you would any fruit-filled morning pastry.*

Preheat the oven to 220°C (425°F) Gas 7.

Place the puff pastry squares on a baking sheet lined with
parchment paper.

Put the sugar and 2 tablespoons of water in a saucepan and bring
to the boil, stirring until the sugar dissolves. Scrape the seeds from
the vanilla bean directly into the sugar syrup, stirring to combine.

Add the apples to the pan, reduce the heat to medium and cook for
4–5 minutes, turning so they cook evenly. Add the blueberries and
gently stir to coat in the sweet syrup. Arrange the apples and
blueberries on top of each pastry square. Bake in the preheated
oven for 18–20 minutes, until the pastry is puffed and golden.

Put the tarts on serving plates. Add a generous spoonful
of cream to each tart and serve immediately.

nectarine & pistachio summer crumble

Crumbles are normally considered to be a comforting winter desserts, but this deliciously light, nutty version makes the most of juicy summer nectarines. It takes very little time to prepare and tastes sublime with ice cream.

Preheat the oven to 220°C (425°F) Gas 7.

To make the crumble topping, put the pistachios and almonds in a food processor and blend until coarsely chopped. Transfer to a bowl. Add the oatmeal and butter and use your fingertips to rub the ingredients together until the mixture resembles coarse, wet sand. Add the flour and sugar and rub together to combine. Cover and refrigerate until needed.

Line a baking sheet with parchment paper. Cut the nectarines in half. If the stone does not come out easily, don't worry – simply slice the flesh off the fruit and drop it directly onto the baking sheet. Sprinkle the crumble topping evenly over the nectarines and bake in the preheated oven for 10–15 minutes, until the fruit is soft and juicy and the topping is a soft golden colour.

Divide the crumble between warmed serving dishes. Add a generous spoonful of cream or ice cream and serve immediately.

70 g/½ cup whole pistachio nuts, coarsely chopped

50 g/⅓ cup blanched whole almonds

60 g/⅔ cup ground oatmeal

50 g/3½ tablespoons cold unsalted butter, cubed

60 g/scant ½ cup plain/all-purpose flour

50 g/¼ cup soft brown sugar

6 nectarines

vanilla ice cream or double/heavy cream, to serve

serves 6

spiced pear trifle

750 ml/3 cups good red wine

150 g/³⁄₄ cup sugar

3 tablespoons clear honey

freshly squeezed juice of 1 lemon

1 cinnamon stick

1 vanilla bean, split lengthways

1 large piece of orange peel

1 whole clove

1 black peppercorn

4–6 firm pears, quartered

300 g/10½ oz. genoese sponge cake
(about one 23–25 cm/9–10 inch cake)

4 tablespoons cognac (optional)

300 ml/1¼ cups ready-made custard

250 ml/1 cup whipping cream,
whipped

toasted flaked almonds

serves 4–6

Trifle is a traditional English dessert, but this recipe departs from the classic version as it uses spiced poached pears instead of canned peaches. It is easy to make and looks spectacular when assembled in a glass serving bowl.

Put the wine, sugar, honey, lemon juice, cinnamon stick, vanilla bean, orange peel, clove and peppercorn in a large saucepan over low heat, stirring occasionally until the sugar has dissolved. Remove from the heat.

Place the pears in the wine mixture and simmer, uncovered, for about 20 minutes or until tender. Set aside until needed.

Cut the sponge cake into pieces and arrange these in the bottom of a glass serving dish. Drizzle with the cognac (if using) and some of the pear poaching liquid. Top with the quartered pears, then spoon over the custard. Spoon the whipped cream on top, sprinkle with the almonds and serve immediately.

baked plums in puff pastry with crème fraîche

This dish can be made with whatever fruit is in season, such as apples, pears or apricots – but plums work particularly well. Be sure to use just-soft plums, not too ripe.

Preheat the oven to 190°C (375°F) Gas 5.

Place the puff pastry squares on a baking sheet lined with parchment paper. Brush with the egg and sprinkle each rectangle very generously with sugar. Bake in the preheated oven until the pastry is puffed and golden.

Cut the plums in half, remove the stones, then slice each half into quarters. Put the plums in a large baking dish, sprinkle with the sugar and bake in the preheated oven for about 20 minutes until tender and slightly browned.

To assemble, split the pastries in half, but not all the way through. Fill with the plums and a generous spoonful of sweetened crème fraîche and serve immediately.

375 g/13 oz. sheet ready-rolled puff pastry, defrosted if frozen, cut into 4 squares each about 12 cm/5 inches square

1 egg, beaten

caster sugar, for sprinkling

6–8 large red plums (not ripe)

50 g/¼ cup sugar

200 g/¾ cup crème fraîche/sour cream, sweetened with 1–2 tablespoons caster sugar

serves 4

crêpes Suzette

110 g/scant 1 cup plain/
all-purpose flour

½ teaspoon salt

1 egg

1 egg yolk

150 ml/⅔ cup milk mixed with
150 ml/⅔ cup water

30 g/2 tablespoons unsalted butter,
melted and cooled

crêpes Suzette sauce

110 g/1 stick unsalted butter

60 g/⅓ cup caster sugar

grated zest and freshly squeezed
juice of 2 oranges

3 tablespoons Curaçao, other citrus
liqueur, or apricot brandy

to finish

1 tablespoon caster sugar

2 tablespoons Curaçao, other citrus
liqueur, or apricot brandy

1 tablespoon dark rum

serves 4 (makes 8–10 crêpes)

*This classic dessert seems to have disappeared in recent years,
but it's still up there with the greats.*

To make the crêpes, put the flour into a food processor, add the salt,
egg, egg yolk, milk and water mixture and cooled melted butter and
blend for a few seconds until smooth. Chill until needed.

Heat a crêpe pan or small frying pan over medium heat, then lightly
brush with butter, using paper towels to wipe away any excess.
Spoon 2 tablespoons of the batter into the hot pan and quickly swirl
it around to coat the base of the pan evenly but thinly. If you add too
much batter just tip the extra back into the bowl and trim away the
pouring trail. Cook the crêpe for 1 minute, then carefully turn it
over and cook the other side.

To make the crêpe Suzette sauce, put the butter, sugar, orange zest
and juice and Curaçao into a large frying pan and gently warm
through over low heat. When the sugar has dissolved, boil the
mixture for 2 minutes to make a butter syrup.

Put the first crêpe into the pan of hot orange butter and, using a
palette knife and fork, fold it into quarters and push it to the edge
of the pan to make room for the next one. Repeat until all the
crêpes are coated in orange butter and folded in the pan.

To finish, keep the pan over very low heat and sprinkle the crêpes
with the sugar, Curaçao and rum. Quickly but very carefully, light
the alcohol in the pan with a match. Serve immediately before the
flames disappear.

grilled peaches with pistachios & dates

A deliciously moreish, easy dessert of peaches stuffed with a creamy, nutritious date and nut filling. The perfect treat for those who don't want to spend long in the kitchen.

Preheat the grill/broiler to medium.

Meanwhile, mix together the cream cheese, orange juice, pistachios and dates in a small bowl.

Cut the peaches in half lengthways, twist to separate the fruit into halves, then prise out the stones.

Spoon the cream cheese mixture into the peach centres. Grill/broil for 6–7 minutes until the cream cheese mixture starts to turn golden and the fruit softens.

2 generous tablespoons low-fat cream cheese

2 teaspoons fresh orange juice (not from concentrate)

10 pistachio nuts or other favourite nuts, roughly chopped

2 stoned dried dates, finely chopped

2 ripe peaches or nectarines

serves 2

chocolate brownie sundae

4 scoops chocolate ice cream

250 ml/1 cup chocolate sauce

4 scoops coffee ice cream

ready-made chocolate brownies

white-and milk-chocolate covered peanuts, to decorate

serves 4

Rich brownies, chocolate ice cream, coffee ice cream studded with chocolate-covered peanuts and lashings of chocolate sauce, make this the ultimate sundae for chocaholics everywhere. It also makes an extra-special treat for any birthday celebration when decorated with sparklers.

Put a square or two of brownie at the base of each sundae dish and top with 1 scoop of chocolate ice cream and 1 scoop of coffee ice cream. Drizzle each sundae with chocolate sauce, top with chocolate-covered peanuts and serve immediately.

roasted mascarpone peaches

Vanilla sugar is easy to make – just put a couple of vanilla beans in a jar of sugar and leave them there, topping up with fresh sugar as necessary.

Preheat the oven to 200°C (400°F) Gas 6.

Cut the peaches in half, remove the stones and arrange the fruit cut side up in a roasting pan. Pour over the honey and bake in the preheated oven for about 20 minutes until soft and lightly golden.

Mix the mascarpone with the vanilla sugar and lemon juice and spoon onto the hot peaches. Divide the peaches between serving plates and serve immediately.

4 large ripe peaches

2 tablespoons clear honey

150 g/²/₃ cup mascarpone

3 tablespoons vanilla sugar

1 tablespoon freshly squeezed lemon juice

serves 4

banana fritters with cinnamon ice cream

2 large bananas

cinnamon ice cream, to serve

ginger batter

40 g/⅓ cup plain/all-purpose flour

a pinch of salt

1 egg, separated

75 ml/¼ cup ginger ale or sparkling water

1 tablespoon sunflower oil, plus extra for deep-frying

serves 4

Fruit fritters are delicious and very simple to make. Cinnamon and banana make an excellent flavour combination, but vanilla or chocolate ice cream would also work well.

Peel the bananas, cut each bananainto 4 chunks, then cut the chunks in half lengthways.

To make the batter, sift the flour and salt into a bowl, beat in the egg yolk, ginger ale or sparkling water and oil to form a smooth batter. Whisk the egg white in a separate bowl until soft peaks form, then fold into the batter.

Heat 5 cm/2 inches sunflower oil in deep saucepan until hot. Dip the banana chunks into the batter and deep-fry in batches of 3–4 for about 1 minute until the batter is crisp and golden. Drain on paper towels and keep them warm while you cook the remainder.

Divide the fritters between serving plates with a scoop of cinnamon ice cream on the side and serve immediately.

bread & butter puddings

These wonderful individual puddings are deliciously creamy and comforting. They are very simple to make and can be cooked in under 20 minutes.

Preheat the oven to 180°C (350°F) Gas 4.

Put the milk, cream, vanilla and 3 tablespoons of the sugar into a saucepan and heat until the sugar dissolves.

Put the eggs into a mixing bowl and whisk well. Stir in 2–3 tablespoons of the hot milk mixture to warm the eggs, then stir in the remainder of the hot milk.

Lightly toast the hot cross buns and cut into quarters. Divide between 6 buttered ramekins and sprinkle with the sultanas.

Pour in the custard, grate a little nutmeg over the top, then sprinkle with the remaining sugar. Bake in the preheated oven for 18–20 minutes until firm. Let cool a little, then serve warm.

300 ml/1¼ cups milk

300 ml/1¼ cups double/heavy cream

½ teaspoon vanilla extract

4 tablespoons caster/granulated sugar

3 eggs

6 hot cross buns, halved

50 g/⅓ cup sultanas/raisins

1 whole nutmeg

serves 6

plum fudge puddings

50 g/3½ tablespoons unsalted butter

50 g/4 tablespoons honey

2 tablespoons double/heavy cream

2 tablespoons soft brown sugar

1 teaspoon ground mixed/apple
pie spice

75 g/1½ cups fresh white breadcrumbs

2 ripe plums, halved, stoned and
thinly sliced

crème fraîche/sour cream, to serve

serves 4

Even if you never make desserts at any other time, you probably do when you have people to dinner. Perfect for such an occasion, these little plum fudge puddings can be prepared in minutes.

Preheat the oven to 200°C (400°F) Gas 6.

Heat the butter, honey and cream in a saucepan over low heat until melted. Put the sugar, spice and breadcrumbs into a bowl and stir well.

Divide half the buttery fudge mixture between 4 ramekins and top with a layer of plum slices and half the breadcrumb mixture. Add the remaining plums and breadcrumbs, then spoon over the remaining sauce.

Set the puddings on a baking sheet and bake in the preheated oven for 20 minutes. Remove from the oven and let cool for 5 minutes, then carefully unmould the puddings onto serving plates. Add a generous spoonful of crème fraîche and serve immediately.

white chocolate pots

This is a simple yet indulgent treat that uses just three ingredients. It's very rich indeed, so just a small portion is all that's needed.

Put the chocolate in a heatproof bowl.

Rub the vanilla bean between your palms to soften it then use a sharp knife to split it open lengthways. Scrape the seeds directly into the bowl with the chocolate.

Set the bowl over a saucepan of barely simmering water, making sure the bottom of the bowl does not come into contact with the water. Let the chocolate slowly melt then remove the bowl from the heat and stir the chocolate until smooth.

Put the mascarpone in a bowl and fold in the melted chocolate.

Spoon the mixture into ramekins or teacups and refrigerate until serving. Serve on its own or with summer berries, if desired.

100 g/²⁄₃ cup good-quality white chocolate, broken into pieces

½ vanilla bean

400 g/1½ cups mascarpone

a selection of fresh summer berries, to serve (optional)

serves 4–6

index

recipe credits

Ross Dobson
pasta salad with roasted peppers, olives & feta
hot smoked salmon & cannellini bean salad with gremolata
Mexican taco salad with pinto beans & avocado
tabbouleh with chickpeas & spring salad
summer vegetable soup with pasta & pistou
swiss chard & white bean minestrone
globe artichoke, tarragon & Roquefort soup
sweet potato & coconut soup with Thai pesto
peppery watercress & pea soup with Gorgonzola
Taleggio & potato tortilla with red pepper tapenade
tenderstem broccoli, shiitake & tofu omelette
penne with spicy meatballs
spaghetti with spicy garlic breadcrumbs
pappardelle with roast fennel, tomato & olives
pasta primavera with lemony breadcrumbs
linguine with tomatoes, red endive & black olives
pappardelle with mushrooms, chestnuts & chives
gnocchetti pasta with smoky Spanish-style sauce
spicy sausage & pepper pizza
wild salmon & sorrel cakes with buttered spring greens
spinach & cheese curry
prosciutto-wrapped fish with walnut pesto & balsamic tomatoes
apple & blueberry tarts
nectarine & pistachio summer crumble
white chocolate pots

Louise Pickford
creamy eggs with goat cheese
charred asparagus & herb frittata with smoked salmon
tuna tartare pasta
pasta with fresh tomato
pasta with melted ricotta & herby Parmesan sauce
seafood fried rice
gingered chicken noodles
cheeseburger
lamb in pita bread

chunky vegetable burgers with pesto
pan-fried chicken with creamy beans & leeks
jerk chicken wings with avocado salsa
warm compote with peaches, apricots & blueberries
roasted mascarpone peaches
banana fritters with cinnamon ice cream
bread & butter puddings
plum fudge puddings

Tonia George
couscous with feta, dill & spring beans
chicken avgolemono
potato, bacon & savoy cabbage soup
smoked haddock & bean soup
sweetcorn & pancetta chowder
rocket soup with poached egg & truffle oil
caramelized chicory with black forest ham & poached eggs
tortilla with potatoes, & roasted pimentos
deep-fried eggs with rice & oyster sauce
tagliatelle with peas & goat cheese pesto
linguine with clams, tarragon & cherry tomatoes
stir-fried asparagus, tofu & peppers with lemongrass, lime leaves & honey
griddled steaks with new potatoes & Roquefort

Caroline Marson
roasted pepper & aubergine salad
beetroot, walnut & warm goat cheese salad
chicken, lemongrass, ginger & rice soup
tom yum seafood noodle soup
Mediterranean chunky fish stew with cheese toasts
tagliatelle with broccoli, anchovy & Parmesan
stir-fried seafood with vegetables & a balsamic dressing
harissa-spiced chickpeas with halloumi & spinach
Spanish sausage & butter bean tagine
tuna steak with warm potato salad & salsa verde
roast figs with honey & marsala

Nadia Arumugam
Buddha's delight
chicken pad Thai
spiced mixed vegetables with cumin & fennel seeds
pork with chilli, Thai sweet basil & toasted coconut
wok-tossed jasmine rice with crabmeat & asparagus
beef chow mein
five-spice duck with plums

Jennie Shapter
smoked salmon omelette
spinach & pancetta frittata
asparagus, pecorino & prosciutto frittata
hearty country-style tortilla
paella tortilla
tortilla with artichokes & serrano ham
spaghetti & tomato frittata

Fiona Smith
pea, prosciutto & pasta salad
bacon, egg & bean salad with grilled chorizo on toast
lemon-rubbed lamb & orzo pasta salad
salade niçoise with fresh tuna
tabbouleh with chickpeas & spring salad
warm chicken livers with watercress & ciabatta

Elsa Petersen-Schepelern
Italian tuna & bean salad
flag bean salad
fresh pea soup with mint & crispy bacon
grilled salmon noodle soup
Thai baby squid with green curry paste

Kimiko Barber
Singapore noodles pages
Shanghai pork noodles
Chiang Mai chicken noodles

Hannah Miles
classic banana split
chocolate brownie sundae

Fran Warde
field mushroom tortilla
seafood curry

Laura Washburn
spiced pear trifle
baked plums in puff pastry with crème fraîche

Ghillie Basan
summer vegetable skewers with homemade pesto

Vatcharin Bhumichitr
stir-fried beef noodles with curry paste

Silvana Franco
herbed tagliatelle with seafood skewers

Nicola Graimes
grilled peaches with pistachios & dates

Kate Habershon
crêpes Suzette

Lindy Wildsmith
warm cherry tomato & mozzarella salad

photography credits

Caroline Arber
Pages 84, 175

Henry Bourne
Page 60

Martin Brigdale
Pages 67, 77, 94, 133, 171-172, 184, 207

Jonathan Buckley
Page 212

Peter Cassidy
Pages 1, 3 (centre; right), 4-5, 6, 11-12, 16, 20-21, 24, 33, 40, 42-43, 45-46, 53, 57-58, 109, 111, 114, 119-120, 132, 137, 138-139, 146, 157, 163, 168-169, 179-180, 183, 187-188, 190-191, 197, 203, 206, 217, 226, 229-231, 233

Nick Dowey
Page 15

Daniel Farmer
Page 202

Tara Fisher
Pages 14, 74, 79, 87, 91-92, 95-96, 99, 101

Jonathan Gregson
Pages 76, 80

Jeremy Hopley
Page 153

Richard Jung
Pages 2, 7, 19, 35, 49, 54-55, 62, 70, 73, 88, 104, 107, 112, 123, 128, 131, 136, 141-142, 144, 154, 158, 161-162, 165, 170, 192, 196, 199-200, 204, 213-214, 224

William Lingwood
Pages 38, 116, 145, 149, 166, 221

Diana Miller
Pages 23, 26-28, 31-32, 36

David Munns
Pages 72, 89, 173, 218

William Reavell
Pages 3(left), 39, 75, 82-83, 121, 124, 127, 150-151, 156, 195, 222

Yuki Sugiura
Pages 41, 50, 61, 65-66, 69

William Shaw
Pages 48, 185

Lucinda Symons
Page 219

Ian Wallace
Pages 100, 103, 126, 209

Kate Whitaker
Pages 8, 106, 108, 115, 135, 176, 178, 205, 210, 225, 234